Superpowe

Indian Worl

History, Politics, Economy and Military of the Indian Subcontinent

Publisher Expertengruppe Verlag

Superpower India – Understanding the Indian World Power

History, Politics, Economy and Military of the Indian Subcontinent

Publisher Expertengruppe Verlag

TABLE OF CONTENTS

ABOUT THE AUTHOR

Hermann Rupold has been living in Hamburg with his wife Charlotte for 4 years. After numerous stations abroad, mainly in Africa, Asia and South America, he has come to rest on the Elbe.

Ever since studying political science more than 25 years ago, he has been dealing with marginal political, social and historical topics that are often hidden from the masses but are widely accepted academically. As a teacher, he not only passes on this knowledge to his pupils and students, but also addresses the broad mass of people in Germany in the context of various publications.

In his books, he is particularly interested in topics where the effects can be felt in many areas of society, but which are nevertheless largely unknown. Moreover, he concentrates on topics where, in addition to general scientific research, his own experiences can be brought to bear. Each of his publications is therefore based not only on indispensable scientific foundations, but also on very personal experiences and insights. These are not only factual in nature, but are also practical works using his broad knowledge and containing useful hints that can be easily understood and followed.

Hermann Rupold creates easy-to-read books that give the reader, in a relaxed and pleasant atmosphere, an insight into subject areas that most people know little about, but from which each individual can benefit greatly.

In this way, he aims above all to arouse curiosity for foreign cultures, to break down preconceptions, and to motivate readers to look beyond their own horizons.

FOREWORD

India - what is that actually? A fabulous subcontinent with a rich culture? The new global Silicon Valley? An emerging country with nuclear weapons, in constant conflict with its arch-enemy Pakistan? Or a new China that is always one step ahead of the established industrial nations thanks to its simple production methods? The fact is: Something is happening in India, and it's happening big. With the dawn of the 21st century, the country has finally shaken off the shackles of former colonial rule and is now going its own way, always on the lookout for niches on the world market to occupy. And it's working: Whether it be microchips or medicines - Indian companies have been able to make a name for themselves in some sectors. Indian corporations are booming on the stock market, giving millions of people jobs and regular incomes. The prosperity is tangible, visible and palpable. Mumbai and New Delhi are economic metropolises and impress with their visible upswing. India has long been considered a promising junior partner on the international economic and political stage. Other nations look with skepticism at the upswing on the subcontinent. The "superpower India" is an uncomfortable concept for the superpower China. Potential for tension is therefore guaranteed. And the other neighbors of the South Asian mega-state? They have long been functioning components of the Indian sphere of interest. If it were not for Pakistan, the hereditary enemy that at some point split off from the originally shared history. Statistically, the country has come out on top in many respects. In India there is a lot of everything. Many people, many faiths, much light and shadow, super rich meet super poor. Luxury medical tourism meets the undersupply of the local population. Peace movements lead to bloody uprisings. And war is always a constant companion for the population of this still young country. India is the largest democracy in the world. But how democratically do people live there? Have the constraints of the notorious caste system really been shaken off? What is certain is that India will soon be the most populous country in the world, leaving China behind in this top position. Is this a good sign in a world full of new challenges like climate change? That remains to be seen. To do that, we need to understand India. And to do that, we need to take a look at the checkered but at the same time fascinating history of this distant country to answer the question: What is the superpower India?

- Chapter 1 -

THE HISTORY OF INDIA

EARLY HISTORY

The Indian subcontinent has been inhabited since the Paleolithic Age. This is proven by a multitude of archaeological finds such as stone hand axes and scraping tools. In 1982, the Indian geologist Arun Sonakia discovered the "Narmada Man" or rather his fossilized skullcap. The man, who lived at least 235,000 years ago, was named after the river of the same name. This was a sensation: for the first time, the fossil of an early man had been found on the subcontinent. Investigations revealed that it was not a man - this was only Sonakia's first assumption. Rather, the skullcap belonged to a woman about 30 years old. She belonged to the species Homo Erectus, an ancestor of modern humans, Homo Sapiens. The first of these modern humans arrived in what is now India between about 73,000 and 55,000 BC. Basically, the African continent is considered the cradle of humanity. In the previously mentioned period, individual groups separated, went on the move and, following the course of the coast, reached India. In the Indus Valley, people gradually began to abandon the nomadic way of life as hunter-gatherers and settle down. Around 5,000 BC, agriculture and animal husbandry intensified. Different types of grain were cultivated and some types of animals such as pigs, goats and oxen were domesticated. This development continued and eventually led to the Indus Civilization, an early but important advanced civilization.

THE INDUS CIVILIZATION

The Indus civilization owes its name to the river of the same name, which rises in Tibet and flows into the Arabian Sea after 3,180 kilometers. The Indus and its widely ramified river system with temporarily flooded plains provided ideal soil for agriculture. However, the Indus civilization was not limited to the banks of the river. The settlement area of this early advanced civilization extended into the Near East, across parts of present-day Pakistan, into the northeastern part of Afghanistan, and covered areas of what is now northwestern India. Together with the Egyptians and Mesopotamians, the Indus culture is considered one of the first significant civilizations in the Bronze Age. The civilization experienced its heyday from 2600 to 1900 BC. With the large cities of Mohenjo-Daro in today's Sindh province in Pakistan and Harappa near Punjab, also in Pakistan, two imposing conurbations emerged. Archaeologists suspect that these metropolises could have housed up to 60,000 inhabitants. Harappa in particular is important to archaeologists. The foundation walls of the city are well preserved and allow conclusions to be drawn about the way of life of the inhabitants. For the technical possibilities of the time, the cities were at an outstanding level of urban development. Thus, there was already a water supply. The construction of the houses and their surroundings, with their characteristic courtyards and fountains, was also a masterpiece of craftsmanship. Even today, corresponding residential complexes can be found in Pakistani and Indian villages, which are strikingly similar to the construction methods of that time. In terms of construction, the cities of the Indus civilization differ from those in other advanced civilizations. While the Egyptians tended to build monumental structures, large buildings are rarely found in the remains of the Indus cities. Buildings of the format of the Egyptian pyramids are completely absent. The largest buildings were probably granaries.

It is considered certain that the inhabitants of the Indus bank were traders and craftsmen. The inhabitants of Harappa fired bricks and pottery and made necklaces, figurines and toys. The inhabitants of Harappa were also skilled in metallurgy: Tin, bronze, lead, and copper were well-known metals. Terracotta figurines decorated with gold were also found. Even mathematics was not an unknown field. Geometric shapes such as cubes were quite well known. A variety of characters were also found on bowls and pots, pointing to a written language. Ultimately, the question of the language of the Indus people has not yet been adequately answered. A conclusive language system could not be identified. The 600 characters discovered could be an artificial language.

The Indus civilization was not a peaceful community. Warlike conflicts took place frequently. This conclusion can be drawn from skeletal finds from Harappa. Clear traces of injuries were found on every sixth skeleton. The existence of diseases such as leprosy could also be proven in this way.

As mentioned, trade was important. So important, in fact, that it is not at all unlikely that the wheel was actually invented within the sphere of influence of the Indus civilization. Archaeological findings indicate that ox carts were in use in early India, and they are still in use today in large parts of southern and eastern Asia. Overland trade benefited from this development. Trade by sea also flourished. That the Indus people traded with the Mesopotamians is considered certain. It is suspected that there may even have been trade relations as far away as Egypt or Crete. But archaeology has not yet been able to provide a real answer to one important question: Who was actually in charge in the land on the Indus? It was unlikely that there was a ruler or “king”, because in the normal case, at least if other advanced civilizations are taken as a yardstick, the regent would have been depicted on images. Corresponding indications have not been found so far. However, researchers are certain that there must have been some form of "superior authority". This is suggested by the sophisticated urban planning. There is the assumption that the cities were led by individuals or by the people themselves. At the very least, it seems that there was a high degree of freedom of decision-making within the individual settlements.

Like every advanced civilization, the time of the Indus civilization also came to an end. Around 1900 BC, the first signs of decay appeared. Obviously, people were leaving the cities. Increasing outbreaks of violence and the spread of serious diseases such as leprosy or tuberculosis could possibly have led to this development. The result was an abandonment of urban locations and a reorientation to a rural and nomadic way of life. An example of this regression can be seen in crafts. Pottery from this period no longer exhibited the once high-quality craftsmanship that was still evident during the heyday of the Indus civilization. Long-distance trade was abandoned and cities fell into disrepair. Newly built houses were "thrown together" rather than expertly constructed. Archaeologists found relics from this period that indicate troubled times. Valuables were found in "hoards", that is, hidden away. This indicates that people of that time were afraid of looting. In addition, bodies were found lying unburied in buildings. Either there had not been time for burial or the inhabitants had not seen a need for it.

THE VEDIC PERIOD

The period between 1900 to 200 BC is called the Vedic period. It is named after the so-called Vedas or Veda, liturgical texts that give us an insight into religious understanding and life culture. After the collapse of the Indus civilization, the Vedic period describes a return to culture. Ancient India was on the upswing again. The Vedas are written in an Indo-Aryan language, which was the forerunner of the language we know today as Sanskrit. Four Vedas are known, the Rigveda, the Yajurveda, the Samaveda and the Atharvaveda, which in turn are divided into a variety of subgroups. One of these is the mantras, which are also known today in Western culture. A mantra is a string of words that are said to have special powers. The Vedas are considered sacred in the Hindu faith, even in the present day. A special feature is the tradition of the Vedas. They were not initially written down, but were transmitted orally, more precisely in songs. The chanting of these Vedas was included in the UNESCO list of Masterpieces of the Oral and Intangible Heritage of Humanity in 2003. Over the centuries, however, numerous copies were made. Thanks to this complicated technique, numerous insights into the way of life of the Indo-Aryan peoples who settled in the north and northwest of India have come down to us today. The Vedas described not only religious themes, but also secular aspects. The Rigveda is considered the oldest text and describes the coexistence of the Indo-Aryans as a pastoral culture and tribal culture. From this text there is not much to see of the earlier achievements of the Indus civilization with its large and modern cities. Life at that time was simple and archaic. In this era, also called the Rigveda period, the Indo-Aryans began to spread into the western part of the Ganges plain, which is located in the northern part of the Indian subcontinent. Furthermore, settlement took place in the Punjab. Insights into the further development are offered by the Atharvaveda, in which a "black metal" is mentioned. Scientists agree that this could only be iron. With that the iron age had begun in India, and things began to change within the communities. Individual tribes first formed associations, i.e. tribal unions, which merged into kingdoms or republics and were called Janapadas. Four such state structures are known: Kuru, Kosala, Panchala and Videha. The latter in particular, Videha, was considered a stronghold of culture and religion.

EXCURSUS: THE ARYANS

The word "Aryans" refers to those people who speak an Indo-Aryan language. In more recent times, the term is also used to refer to Indo-Iranian, a language that was widely spoken in the Bronze Age and Copper Age. The homeland of the Aryans was Ariana; at least this is how the Romans and Greeks referred to the area of land that is now largely the national territory of Afghanistan.

This Indo-Aryan language is - simply put - related to Germanic. In 19th century Europe, this led to a stylization of the Aryans as the "original people", combined with the idea that they belonged to the same ethnic group. Among the scholars of the time, the idea grew that the Aryan race was superior to the others. An idea that was later taken up and further radicalized by the National Socialists in Germany. In his book Mein Kampf, Adolf Hitler further shaped the idea that Germans, as descendants of the Aryans, were not only superior, but that their continued existence was threatened by so-called "racial mixing". This belief laid the foundation for the Nazis' horrific crimes.

In the context of ancient Indian history, the term is rarely used. Instead, the term Indo-Aryan is used.

Basically, the settlement of northern India by the Indo-Aryans, who had their original home in the grassy steppes to the northwest, proceeded slowly. In the late Vedic period, a caste system emerged that continues to play an important role in modern India and the Hindu belief system. Castes were divided into Brahmins (priests), Kshatriyas (warriors), Vaishyas (peasants), Shudras (subjects), and Pariahs (casteless). In the same era, society was changing. Cities were founded and people abandoned their nomadic way of life. There was an increase in agriculture. Rice was cultivated on a large scale. The aforementioned tribal unions, republics and kingdoms flourished, new ones were added, and others merged. By 600 BC, there were 16 such kingdoms. The most important was the kingdom of Magadha with its king Bimbisara, who pursued a successful trade and expansion policy and established a functioning administration. About 80,000 villages and settlements are said to have belonged to this kingdom. This number, however, is probably due to the imagination of the chroniclers. At almost the same time (563 BC), Siddhartha Gautama was born in Lumbini in northern Magadha. The son of a prince went down in history under the name Buddha.

THE CLASSICAL AGE OF INDIA

Around 400 BC, the Nanda Empire was founded in Magadha, which encompassed almost the entire north of present-day India. The empire was considered very modern and yet very short-lived. The Nanda dynasty became extinct shortly after the invasion of India by the Greek or Macedonian general Alexander the Great and was succeeded by Chandragupta Maurya. This is considered the birth of the Maurya Empire, one of the largest and most powerful state entities in the history of the subcontinent, which also originated in Magadha. Chandragupta fought against Alexander's troops who had been left in the Indus Valley after his campaign. It was not only as a general that the first king of Maurya made a name for himself. He was considered a skillful diplomat who negotiated elaborate treaties with the Greek military leader. Under Chandragupta's grandson Ashoka, the Maurya Empire reached its heyday and greatest expansion. It is said to have covered an area of 5 million square kilometers and had a population of about 60 million. This would have made Maurya the most populous state in the ancient world. Ashoka was ideologically ahead of his time. He converted to Buddhism and made the principle of peace the doctrine of the state. Violence was rejected and conflicts were settled peacefully. Emphasis was also placed on helping those in need. His rule describes a form of governance that was unknown in the great European empires of antiquity.

Brihadratha was a grandson of Ashoka and the last representative of the Maurya dynasty. In 185 BC, he was deposed by his general Pushyamitra and the Maurya dynasty was extinguished. This "coup" marked the beginning of the Shunga kingdom, about which, however, hardly any details have survived. This kingdom had two major metropolises, Pataliputra and Vidisha. Very little information has been handed down about this period, making it the subject of much speculation. In 73 B.C., the incumbent king Devabhuti was assassinated by a slave on the orders of his minister Vasudeva. This cleared the way for him to head the empire. This was followed by the very short Kanva dynasty, which lasted only 45 years. The proof that this line of rulers existed at all is only provable thanks to the mention in the Puranas, the holy scriptures in Hinduism. Furthermore, coins minted during the Kanva dynasty have been found. By this time, the empire was no longer as extensive as it used to be. The national territory disintegrated, at least partially, into separate kingdoms and principalities. The Kanva dynasty was dissolved by the Satavahana, who built up their own empire in the central Indian highlands from 230 BC. The Satavahana were also known as Andhras, indicating that they originated in the region of the same name. Andhra Pradesh is still a state of India today. Due to the conquerors from central India, the once important Magadha was reduced to a city on the periphery of the Satavahana Empire, the center of which was the present-day city of Nashik with a population of over a million. The Satavahana Empire was considered modern. The rulers supported both Brahmins and Buddhists financially. Banking also experienced an upswing. For example, the Satavahana established interest rates. The empire lasted until about 220 A.D. As late as the 2nd century, its influence in central India grew considerably, for example, through its merger with neighboring Maharashtra, but it dwindled just as quickly. Conflict was brewing with the Sakas, who inhabited the steppes of northeast India and central Asia as nomads. They were considered vassals of the Kushan Empire, a great empire in the northeastern part of India, which in its greatest expansion around 250 AD reached as far as present-day China. The rulers of Kushana, Indo-European nomads, also came from the Yuezhi province there. This epoch is classified by Indian historiography as a "dark age" because Kushans were perceived as foreign rulers. The adoption of the Greek alphabet was also seen as a sign of foreign domination. Nevertheless, the Kushan form of government brought prosperity to the region. There were rich trade relations with China, and there were also diplomatic contacts with Rome, which were not always untroubled. Roman officials complained about the fact that the Kushans did not produce their own coins, but had Roman sestertii minted. These coins already bore the designation "Maharaja" as a ruler's title. This was a nuisance for the tight administrative system of the Romans. Not only the Kushan Empire, but also the Satavahana Empire maintained close trade contacts with the Roman Empire. Exports were mainly luxury goods: ivory, precious stones, silk, spices and fragrant perfumes went from northeast India and south India to central Europe. The balance of trade was far from balanced. There was no comparable demand in India for Roman trade goods such as glass or copper, so the Romans paid for the imported goods with gold coins, which met the above-mentioned fate and thus disappeared from the financial cycle. This negative balance caused a real economic crisis in Rome, among other places. Why the Kushan Empire was ultimately doomed to decline around 250 AD remains hidden even to modern historians.

EXCURSUS: THE MAHARAJA

In the feudal system of India's past, there was an incomprehensible number of noble titles and predicates. Probably the best-known title of Hindu noble lines is the Maharajah. "Raja" is the most important part of the title here and means "king". The "Maha" means "great" - thus the Maharaja is a great king. However, the plainer title "Raja" was more commonly used. It is interesting that each male scion of the raja was allowed to have his own title. And there was usually a large number of them. The eldest son of a raja was called the crown prince Rajkumar, the second born was called Diwan, the third born was called Thakur, the fourth born Lal and the fifth son Babu. There were probably no special names for daughters, but there certainly were for female rulers. If a woman sat on the throne, she was called Rani or Maharani.

The Satavahana came into conflict with the nomadic Saka, who were themselves vassals of the Kushan Empire. Although the Satavahana defeated the Saka, the succession period was marked by unrest. At the beginning of the 3rd century, the empire disintegrated into several principalities. The "Golden Age" followed. For the immediate successors of the Satavahana were the Gupta dynasty and its counterweight, the Vakatakas.

The Gupta Empire lasted from about 320. AD to 550 AD and, together with Maurya and Kushana, is considered the epitome of Indian antiquity. After the disintegration of the Kushan and Satavahana empires, India was ruled by many states and there was no unity. The kings of Gupta, who came from Bengal in northeastern India, succeeded in reunifying the political patchwork. The name of the founder of the dynasty was Chandragupta I. However, this statement should be treated with caution, as the surviving sources (for example, on coins) merely do not mention any other potential rulers before Chandragupta. Little is known about his reign, apparently he resided in Patna, which today is a city of nearly two million inhabitants. Far more details are known about his son

Samudragupta, who made a name for himself as a successful general. Through numerous campaigns, he unified the previously politically fragmented subcontinent. Inscriptions on stone pillars show that he conducted campaigns in Sri Lanka and northern Iran. An important propaganda tool at the time were coins stylizing Samudragupta as a real hero. Images on gold coins show him not only as an accomplished general, but also as an artist. He gave himself the title Maharajahiraja Paramabhattaraka, which loosely translated means "Great King of Kings". For the Gupta dynasty, coins and titles were an important part of legitimation.

Despite Samudragupta's successes and conquests, the Gupta empire was not yet a great power, but it did provide political stabilization through the unification of the autonomous principalities. The empire became a real empire only under Samudragupta's son, Chandragupta II. In addition to military strength, he brought another means of maintaining power into play: diplomacy. Through clever and purposeful marriages, he created proximity to the rival Vakataka dynasty, who had created an empire of considerable size in southern India. Chandragupta II gave his daughter in marriage to the southern empire. Henceforth, Gupta and Vakataka formed a kind of alliance. For Chandragupta II, the pacification of the south was important: other enemies were waiting in the northeast in the form of the nomadic Shakas, whose subjugation was an explicit goal. The Gupta ruler also wanted to extend his sphere of influence to the West Indies.

Contemporary chroniclers who described everyday life in the Gupta Empire of that time praised Chandragupta in the highest terms. Merchants and officials became enormously wealthy due to the ruler's domestic skills, and art and culture flourished. During this period, several important buildings such as temples were erected, which still exist today. Hinduism experienced a new renaissance, and Buddhism came under increasing competitive pressure.

Chandragupta II ruled until about 415 AD, and his successor, Kumaragupta, continued on the path of prosperity. Under his reign, which was described as particularly mild, trade, art and culture flourished. Both religious currents, Buddhism and Hinduism, developed, yet massive difficulties arose under Kumaragupta. There was a widely convoluted administrative system comparable to federalism. Kumaragupta had comparatively less say for a king. Provincial lords could rule over their territories with virtually no influence from above. As a result, tax revenues were no longer passed on to the king, but were embezzled by officials. The Guptas lost more and more power. In addition to these internal political difficulties, a new enemy was pushing at the borders of the empire at the end of the 5th century, called the "Iranian Huns", a rather loose group of Central Asian tribes. These are not the Huns of European historiography. However, which ethnic group these tribes really comprised of is disputed. It is considered likely that they were the Alchon people, who would also play a role in the future of the Gupta. Skandagupta, the son of Kumaragupta, was able to stop the enemies a few times, but the Gupta empire was already doomed. In the defensive struggle, further expansion was impossible. Some regions openly sought independence. When Skandagupta's nephew, Budhagupta, took over as head of the empire in about 476 AD, the Gupta empire still existed within its old borders. Thereafter followed a period of political turmoil without a unified successor. According to inscriptions, there were nearly 500 different people in the empire who called themselves (regional) kings. The "main throne" of the empire became the subject of numerous disputes. Exactly who was the king of the Gupta Empire at what time during this phase cannot be determined.

At the beginning of the 6th century, the Alchon again invaded Indian territory. This time the defensive struggle turned out to be problematic. The Alchon conquered Punjab and Kashmir and the most important (and last) pretender to the throne of the Gupta Empire suffered a crushing defeat with his army and had to flee. These severe military defeats, combined with the loss of significant territories, finally heralded the end of the Gupta dynasty. Last attempts to repel the Alchon invasion were in vain and the empire again disintegrated into many individual principalities. By the middle of the 6th century, resistance was finally broken and the Alchon ruled the land.

THE INDIA OF THE MIDDLE AGES

Around the year 590 AD Harshavardhana was born, also known as Harsha, who subsequently rose to become one of the most famous regents of (north) India. Harsha was a descendant of the Vardhanas and was born during the period of polyarchy and Alchon occupation. His father, a general of the eliminated Gupta dynasty, fought against Alchon and some seditious princes. The Alchon, on the other hand, were not a homogeneous group internally and were themselves affected by disintegration. Through clever alliances and marriages, Harsha's father was able to gain some influence that paved the way to the crown. Harsha's brother Rajya was supposed to take over, but he fell victim to a plot and was murdered. So it was Harsha's task to ascend the throne. The conspirator who initiated Rajya's murder was the king of Bengal, Shashanka. Harsha moved in with a large army and forced Shashanka to sign a treaty. Subsequently, Harsha achieved further military successes. He took control in Kannauj and conquered Sindh, Vallabhi, Kashmir, Magadha and Gujarat. War followed war and within just six years Harsha was able to bring an empire with an extension of 3,000 kilometers under his control. This was the birth of a gigantic empire that encompassed the entire present-day territory of India. Practically, Harsha had eliminated all his enemies at that time. Only his old adversary Shashanka withstood the attempts at conquest. It was only when the Bengal king died around 620 AD that this empire also dissolved by Harsha. Harsha, who is still a famous figure in Indian history, was not always successful in his drive for expansion. For example, a conquest of the Indus Valley and the west coast of India failed. Nevertheless, Harsha succeeded in establishing a monumental empire.

In the central part of India, however, other powerful people ruled at that time: the Chalukya and the Pallava. The two families competed for dominance in this region. The Chalukya came to power twice in the course of time: between 550 and 750 AD, and between 973 and 1190 AD. King Pulakeshin II gained particular notoriety for resolutely opposing an attempted conquest by Harsha. Instead of an invasion, a peace treaty was reached. Pulakeshin, who resided in his capital Vatapi, today's small town of Badami, felt safe, as the city was considered impregnable, at least until the faithful of the rival Pallava Empire successfully besieged the city and assassinated Pulakeshin.

The Chalukya, who ruled more of the western part of central India, engaged in merciless battles with Pallava, who ruled more of the eastern part. The borders of the empires overlapped through conquests and reconquests. The Chalukya Empire, which lasted until around the year 750 AD, was finally overrun by another dynasty, the Rashtrakuta. The Pallava Empire did not meet a peaceful fate either. After a bitter civil war, the empire was repeatedly threatened by foreign powers. In just under 150 years, the capital Kanchipuram was conquered a total of three times: once by the Chalukya and twice by the Rashtrakuta.

In the centuries from 800 to 1000 AD, three powers divided the Indian subcontinent: The Rashtrakuta, the Pala, and the Pratihara. The Rashtrakuta ruled the central part of India, the Pala Bengal, and the Pratihara the northeastern part of India. The three powers were in permanent conflict with each other. In particular, the ancient capital Kannauj was the subject of numerous disputes. In the long run, however, none of the three great powers could maintain their military conquests. In cultural terms, too, little happened in this era. Life took place mainly in the villages and there was a system of tribute. The Middle Ages in India are thus comparable to the conditions in the European Middle Ages. The many individual principalities possessed a great degree of self-sufficiency. Thus, regional rulers often raised their own armies and collected tax revenues. Whether these revenues actually reached the kings was in turn dependent on the loyalty of the local vassals. There were also many self-sufficient village communities that operated independently of the imperial administration. These communities were presided over by councils that established, for example, local judicial and economic systems. Basically, social development stagnated, and the Middle Ages in India was considered an era of stagnation. In religious terms, the importance of Buddhism in society declined and Hinduism gained strength.

Nevertheless, this period saw the flourishing of one of the most important Indian empires: The Chola Empire. The dynasty of the same name was already established in southern India during Ashoka's time, but it took a long time for the empire to strengthen. One impetus was initially the disintegration of the Pallava Empire, which initially promised a boost. Nevertheless, due to their militarily strong neighbors, the Cholas were initially unable to expand their sphere of influence beyond the borders of their capital Thanjavur. In their attempts at expansion, victories and defeats alternated regularly. This situation changed only when King Rajaraja I, who was considered an accomplished general, came to power. Rajaraja defeated the hostile kingdoms in the neighborhood. He also managed to successfully invade Sri Lanka. Rajaraja's son, Rajendra, also distinguished himself as an accomplished general, surpassing his father's conquests. He captured the capital of the Chalukya Empire and subsequently conquered the Pallava capital. The geographical extent of his undertakings was particularly impressive. He led his forces across the sea to Sri Vijava, a great Buddhist empire whose heartland was Sumatra and which extended to Java. He also maintained relations with China. Subsequently, the Chola Empire continued to flourish, but was weakened by internal political disputes that resulted in civil wars. Around the middle to end of the 13th century, the Chola Empire was destroyed by the competing Pandya dynasty from southern India.

THE ISLAMIC EMPIRES IN INDIA

For a long time, the Indian kingdoms in the north and northeast of the subcontinent had to defend themselves against Muslim invaders. The first attacks took place as early as the 8th century. Attempts at invasion reached a climax at the end of the 12th century. The Ghurids, a Muslim people from Ghur in what is now central Afghanistan, faced the Rajputs on several occasions. The Rajputs were a type of knightly tribe whose members were recruited from the warrior caste, the Kshatriya. The Rajputs were considered honorable warriors and this was to be their undoing. Trapped in a complicated code of honor and outdated warfare, the Rajputs had little to oppose the Ghurids. The Ghur warriors relied on their first-rate mounted army, which was far superior to the war elephants of the Rajputs. Nevertheless, the battles were marked by iron determination, but also terrible cruelty. The resistance was of little use: after 1192, the entire north came under Muslim rule. This also meant the end of Buddhism in India.

The first Muslim empire on the territory of present-day India originated from the so-called slave dynasty. The name comes from the origin of the founder of the dynasty. Qutb-ud-Din Aibak was a former slave who held the position of a commander under Muizz ad-Din Muhammad. After the conquests in India, the Ghurid Muhammad died without an heir. Aibak was able to assert himself after internal power struggles and thus became the sultan of the new Delhi Sultanate in 1206. His reign ended in a rather unspectacular way: Qutb-ud-Din Aibak died after only four years at the head of the sultanate as a result of an accident during a polo match. The new sultan subsequently became Aram Shah, who was ousted from his throne only a year later by Shams ud-Din Iltutmish, Aibak's son-in-law. His reign saw tough fighting in northern India, which was beyond the reach of the slave dynasty. The battles lasted 17 years, but ended successfully for Iltutmish, who subsequently distinguished himself as a religiously tolerant ruler. Due to changes in the rules of succession, his daughter Radiyya ascended the throne in 1236. This is a peculiarity in the Muslim-influenced part of Indian history: for female rulers were extremely rare. Her fate, however, ended tragically. Radiyya was deposed and murdered. From 1242, the rulers of the Delhi Sultanate changed several times. Several sons of Iltutmish took turns at the helm. In 1265, a turning point in history occurred. The former slave Balban became sultan and ruled his country by force. Nevertheless, Balban had a lucky hand as a military leader and was able to conquer Lahore, for example. However, he did not succeed in something crucial: and that was the successful arrangement of a succession. Balban's next male descendants were killed by force, so that his line became extinct. Subsequently, Jalal ud-Din, commander-in-chief of the military, occupied the throne and founded the Khaliji dynasty. His own nephew Ala ud-Din Khalji assassinated him and became Sultan himself. Ala ud-Din Khaliji succeeded in repelling the Mongols, who invaded the sultanate and advanced as far as Delhi in 1299 and 1303. To defend his empire, the sultan recruited a massive cavalry, in which 500,000 soldiers are said to have served. This militarization was costly, and Ala ud-Din Khaliji raised the needed funds from the people. He virtually expropriated the private property of the citizens and even valuables such as gold were taken from the residents of the Delhi Sultanate. In addition, farmers had to surrender half of their harvest. In the end, Ala ud-Din fared like many cruel rulers in history: He was killed when he was most vulnerable - namely on his deathbed. An unnamed son took the throne after the death of the sultan, who was also murdered after a comparatively short time. Thus, the short-lived Khaliji dynasty also came to an abrupt and brutal end in 1320. The new sultan of Delhi was Ghiyas-ud-din Tughluq, the former governor of Punjab. He distinguished himself by providing a milder reign than his predecessor(s) and established the Tughluq dynasty, the last powerful dynasty of the Delhi Empire. Under his rule, agriculture in the sultanate flourished anew and taxes were reduced. Ghiyas-ud-Din died in an accident: a pavilion collapsed and buried the sultan. At least that is how it seemed. However, the collapse was a disguised assassination attempt, cleverly engineered by his son Muhammad bin Tughluq. Muhammad inherited his father's throne in 1325. The new sultan was described by contemporaries as educated and highly intelligent, but also unworldly and unscrupulous. A lot of blood was shed under his rule. Muhammad succeeded in conquering all of India - with a few exceptions such as the southernmost tip of the subcontinent - but also suffered disastrous defeats. When he sent his armies on a campaign to Tibet, his soldiers apparently underestimated the climatic conditions in the Himalayas and were completely wiped out - an absolute disaster. Domestically,

Muhammad was also known for his questionable decisions and moved the capital of the Sultanate from Delhi to Deogir, which still exists today under the name Daulatabad and is a village of about 6,500 people. And even in Muhammad's time, this place was not a center of power. In order to give the place more abundance, the inhabitants of Delhi were relocated there. But even the increased population did not bring the desired "capital city flair" - Deogir was abandoned and Delhi became the new old capital. Bad decisions in the army leadership, the relocation of the capital and a naive financial policy led to revolts and the decline of the Delhi Sultanate. Numerous individual states or kingdoms became independent. When Muhammad tried to put down an uprising in Sindh with his soldiers, he fell seriously ill and eventually died in 1351, succeeded by his cousin Firuz Shah. Firuz is considered to have been comparatively lenient: Thus, he compensated those of his subjects who were victims of Muhammad's crimes. He also abolished the death penalty and emerged as a great builder.

EXCURSUS: THE BUILDINGS OF FIRUZ SHAH

Firuz Shah was the last sultan of the Delhi Empire who had real importance. During his reign, mosques and temples were built. And he even had his own capital - Firuzabad - built. Some of these buildings are still standing today. For many buildings, of course, this is no longer the case. However, since Firuz himself participated in many construction projects and also left an extensive autobiography, a written record of his buildings has survived. Thus, he is said to have been involved in the construction of 20 palaces, 50 dams, 100 "hospitals" and 100 baths. Of course, Firuz set himself an architectural monument with a magnificent mausoleum. This still stands today quite close to Delhi.

As mentioned, Firuz was the last notable sultan of Delhi. He was followed by a few more insignificant sultans from the Tughluq line. The significant turning point in the Delhi Empire was marked in 1398, when Timur Lenk, the famous leader of a Turku-Mongol tribe from Samarkand in present-day Uzbekistan, conquered and ransacked Delhi. The sultanate initially remained in place. But more and more regions became independent of the Delhi Empire, whose power was concentrated only in the capital. An unsteady period full of chaos followed. Slowly but surely, the Sayyid dynasty rose to the top of power. The family saw its claim to power as clearly legitimate: After all, they considered themselves direct descendants of the Prophet Muhammad. In their 37-year reign over the remnants of the Delhi Sultanate, the Sayyids provided four rulers, but they were under the influence of the descendants of Timur Lenk. They were considered weak, incompetent rulers. On April 19, 1451, the last Sayyid sultan abdicated, clearing the way for the Lodi dynasty, which originated in Afghanistan. The first ruler of this line was Bahlul Lodi. His time was determined by numerous military operations, sometimes for conquest, sometimes for defense. Bahlul's son, Sikandar, succeeded him and ruled from 1489 to 1517. As with his father, Sikandar's time as sultan was marked by warlike conflicts. A new and modern administrative system was established in Delhi. In short, Delhi experienced a final period of prosperity, and culture and literature were held in high esteem at this time. This contrasts with the time of Ibrahim Lodi, the last Sultan of Delhi. Under Ibrahim's reign, the empire disintegrated once again. It was marked by internal strife. The death blow, however, came from outside. Among others, it was Ibrahim's uncle Alam Khan who made common cause with Babur

Khan, the Mongol ruler of Kabul in present-day Afghanistan, and betrayed Ibrahim. And more than that, Babur was encouraged by Ibrahim's people to invade Delhi with his army. This led to the First Battle of Panipat on April 20, 1526. The clash is of great historical significance. For one thing, the battle marked the first time in India that firearms such as cannons were used in significant numbers. For another, Ibrahim was killed in battle. This not only led to the extinction of the Lodi line. With Ibrahim died the last Sultan of Delhi. Babur Khan did not think of leaving Delhi again after the conquest and founded the Mughal Empire.

THE MUGHAL EMPIRE

The Mughal Empire, founded by Babur Khan, was one of the longest-lived and largest empires on the Indian subcontinent. It existed from 1526 to 1858, and at the height of its power at the end of the 17th century, it extended over almost all of India as well as significant parts of what is now Afghanistan. After the successful battle of Panipat, the elimination of Ibrahim Lodi and with it the entire Delhi Sultanate, Babur had himself crowned "Emperor of Hindustan", thereby laying the foundation for the Mughal Empire. It is believed that the title Mughal was first used for the ruler of India by the Portuguese in the 16th century.

After the capture of Delhi and the city of Agra in northern India, Babur Khan's empire initially stood on shaky ground. Even though the former sultanate was shattered, the other independent empires in the neighboring regions threatened its stability. It took another year, until 1527, before Babur was able to secure his empire and expand his power through several campaigns against competing rulers. To his new subjects, Babur presented himself as a mild, generous and lavish ruler who always showered his followers with costly gifts. So costly, in fact, that the gifts brought the state treasury to the brink of bankruptcy. Despite these accounts, Babur Khan was considered a determined ruler. He adopted the old system of the extinct Lodi dynasty. His love for gardening is still visible today. When he died in 1530, he had himself buried in the "Bagh-e Babur", the Garden of Babur, a magnificent green space complete with mausoleum.

He was succeeded by his son Humayun, who was unable to build on his father's success. The conditions for the assumption of state power were already problematic. In the Timurid line of succession, that is, the successors of Timur Lang, to which Babur and his sons belonged, the right to the throne was not only granted to the firstborn. All male descendants of the previous mogul had a right to rule. Humayun was thus always involved in fights with his brothers over the legitimacy of power. This severely disturbed the internal balance of power, and at times Humayun had no power over his kingdom at all. His character also had an impact on the rather shaky empire: Humayun was considered fickle and even childish at times. The mogul spent a lot of time drawing up plans for a new capital. Successful campaigns were rare, although they would have been necessary. This was because some Indian rulers refused to be loyal to him and openly rebelled against Humayun, including Sultan Bahadur of Gujarat in the far west of what is now India and Sher Khan Suri in the east, who sought to rebel with a group of former soldiers of the Lodi dynasty. Humayun became embroiled in a struggle on two fronts. At first, he succeeded in further conquests in Gujarat. But the rebellion under Sher Khan Suri forced him to turn his focus eastward and abandon the territories he had just captured in western India. The struggle was unsuccessful. Sher Khan's troops inflicted heavy defeats on Humayun's army. Gradually, more cities in the Mughal Empire were conquered. The only way out for Humayun was to flee into exile. It was not until 1545 that he was able to regain Kabul. However, he was only able to do so with the support of Persian soldiers. Nevertheless, Humayun could not return to India until 1554. In the meantime, the successful field army Sher Kahn Suri founded a short-lived empire and called himself Sultan. Uncertainty about a possible succession led to unrest in the sultanate, which Humayun exploited and took power again. The Mughal Empire was thus restored.

Humayun's son Akbar became the new ruler of the empire, and one of the greatest and most important figures in Indian history. At first, the new regent was controversial, but he quickly consolidated his power due to military successes. In the second battle of Panipat, Akbar defeated the Hindu general Hemu, a subordinate of the Surids and thus a competitor for power in India. Hemu and his soldiers briefly occupied Delhi. At that time, the Surids ruled parts of northern India and aspired to overall power. In the second Panipat battle, Hemu was defeated, killed and beheaded. Had this not happened, Hemu would have claimed dominion over the Mughal Empire for the Surids. This important victory had great significance for the following period as well: Akbar's Mughal Empire became the major military force in the region, thereby consolidating its power. After the victory against Hemu, Akbar was also able to conquer Delhi and Agra, both times with little resistance.

EXCURSUS: THE COURAGEOUS AKBAR

Akbar was considered an exceptionally courageous and cunning commander. In quite a few battles, he is said to have fought at the front line and at the risk of his life. He also made use of numerous tricks: In the second battle of Panipat, he is said to have succeeded in stealing the entire stock of the enemy's cannons. A move that decisively influenced the course of the battle. In the case of a victorious duel, he was considered a generous winner. He often let his defeated opponents leave alive. Thus, in the future, the opponents were in his debt and were bound to Akbar for reasons of honor. Accordingly, the young mogul refrained from cutting off the head of the defeated general Hemu. The reason: Hemu had received an arrow in his left eye, which emerged out of the back of his head. Since Akbar did not want to kill a defenseless and severely wounded man, one of the mogul's comrades took over this task.

After Akbar's sphere of influence had grown significantly, he did not rest. Numerous successful conquests followed and his empire continued to grow. In 1568, he succeeded in finally defeating the Rajputs. No Muslim ruler in India had ever achieved this before. He also managed to integrate the followers of the warrior caste into his army, who would henceforth be an important pillar of his army. Subsequently, he focused more on strengthening his power internally. Consequently, he brought the administrative reforms, which had been sought by Sher Khan Suri, to a successful conclusion. In the process, he showed himself to be exceptionally liberal, especially in religious matters. He succeeded in integrating Hindus more strongly into everyday life and work. Hindus became more and more equal citizens, insofar as one could speak of equality at all at that time. After all, special taxes for Hindus were abolished, which at least brought some relief. Akbar himself moved away from the conservative Muslim faith. This alienation even went so far that Akbar proclaimed his own religion for a time. His social reforms were far more secular: he forbade the marriage of children. The feudal system was also abolished and replaced by a comparatively modern administrative apparatus. However, the officials under Akbar were considered so corrupt that some reforms could never really be implemented.

Akbar's departure from the strict interpretation of the Muslim faith caused problems. This development was a thorn in the side of conservative scholars. Akbar's half-brother Hakim incited them to start a rebellion against their mogul. A dicey situation developed for

Akbar, because Hakim's followers were numerous. Only a successful occupation of Kabul in 1581 ended Hakim's revolt. Through far-sighted diplomacy and foreign policy, Akbar succeeded in ushering in a period of stability. The empire now included the entire north of present-day India, as well as parts of Pakistan and Afghanistan. When Akbar died in 1605, he left behind an empire that had been consolidated both internally and externally, with a modern administrative system. Akbar's India was the undisputed power in southern Asia. The successful line of his father was continued almost unchanged by the heir to the throne, Selim, called Jahangir. Laws on inheritance were reformed, and personal property was better protected under Jahangir's rule. The last remaining enemies were bound to the Mughal Empire, so the period of peace continued. He was succeeded by Shah Jahan, the son of Jahangir.

Shah Jahan, one of the most magnificent rulers in the history of the Mughal Empire, reigned from 1628. He particularly promoted architecture and had buildings erected that still shape India's image in the world today, such as the famous Taj Mahal. However, the magnificent buildings cost the Mughal Empire a fortune. The situation was so serious that extreme inflation threatened. The following period was characterized by a large number of campaigns, most of which were not really successful and were also enormously costly. There was also pressure from outside: neighboring Persia was steadily developing into a great power, and this caused tensions. Disagreements also dominated the internal situation of the Mughal Empire under Shah Jahan. Moreover, trouble loomed especially in the last years of Shah Jahan's reign. His son Aurangzeb took the throne after bloody disputes with his brothers.

After the takeover, the empire fell into decline. His expansionist policy - Aurangzeb continued to expand his empire in southern India - was only superficially successful. Rather, military efforts again led to a massive shortage of money. Nevertheless, the empire expanded inexorably and by 1700 encompassed the entire subcontinent except for the southern tip of India and Sri Lanka. Aurangzeb put the greatest effort into this expansion, which meant that he neglected to focus on the older part of the Mughal Empire in northern India. In addition, Aurangzeb was considered a religiously intolerant theocrat and based his claim to power on Islam. Hindus suffered greatly under his rule. This created tensions. Many of the principalities under Aurangzeb were Hindu. In many places, the tension escalated into bloody revolts against Aurangzeb, who had to fight bitterly for his power throughout his life. The only thing that held the empire together was Aurangzeb's personal authority, for he fundamentally did not trust his advisors, such as army leaders and ministers. During Aurangzeb's time, an additional threat blossomed in the south and west of India in the form of the Maratha Empire.

Basically, after his death in 1707, Aurangzeb left behind a shattered empire the decline of which seemed unstoppable. Bahadur Shah, son of Aurangzeb and his successor, also failed in this attempt. Some regions split off from the Mughal Empire, which Bahadur Shah had to accept idly. He assumed the throne at an advanced age and died after only five years of rule in 1712. His son Jahandar Shah already failed in his attempt to maintain order in the empire and was killed after eight months in office. He was succeeded by Farrukh Siyar, a Sayyid who was allied with the Maratha and whose puppet he was considered to be. It was Farrukh Siyar who made considerable concessions to a new power: the British. Already in previous years, the British had a presence on the Indian coast. By 1700, Madras, Calcutta and Bombay had become important ports. The French maintained similarly important foreign trade posts in Pondicherry and the Portuguese in Goa.

EXCURSUS: EARLY TRADING POSTS OF EUROPEAN STATES OTHER THAN GREAT BRITAIN IN INDIA

India was not only of interest to the British. Other, imperialist powers also had their eye on the country, which promised brisk trade. The French, for example, settled in Pondicherry. This was done without violence: the small fishing village was bought from the local sultan and subsequently developed into a hub of French overseas trade. In 1947, there was a referendum among the citizens, all of whom were French citizens after the 1948 revolution. The question of whether Pondicherry should remain part of the French state was answered in the affirmative by a majority. In the years that followed, however, Indian nationalists gained influence, so that Pondicherry passed to India in 1954. Other lands under French control in

India were Yanam, Karaikal, Mahe and Chandannagar.

The Portuguese also established bases in India. The territory comprised three unconnected tracts of land. The most important settlement was Goa, which was conquered in 1510. Not only was it an important trading post for the export of expensive goods such as spices, Goa was considered a kind of "headquarters" for the Portuguese world empire. From there, the Portuguese overseas territories in Africa and in wider Asia were also administered. Fourteen years after India's independence, troops invaded Goa. The Portuguese capitulated and Goa became part of the Indian state.

There was also a colony called Dutch India. However, it was not located in what is now India, but in Indonesia.

Farrukh endowed the British with broad powers to expand trade. For example, merchants from Britain were exempted from customs duties. Farrukh hoped this would stimulate foreign trade, but this plan quickly backfired: Due to the British trade monopoly, the

Indians quickly became economically dependent on the empire, which knew how to exploit this very well. Even the provinces of the Mughal Empire could only be held by concessions that turned them into semi-autonomous states. Farrukh found himself in a difficult position. He was severely criticized for his unsuccessful style of government and was eventually assassinated by the Sayyids who had once brought him to office and who had played a major role in India's history as far back as three hundred years. As a result, a power struggle broke out, but the Sayyids were unable to win it. The new mogul was Muhammad Shah, who, apart from executing the Sayyids competing for the throne, had few important milestones during his reign. The administrative structures became fragile. This led to the revolution of the Deccan province, which was driven primarily by Muhammad's former vizier - a high government official in the Mughal era - Asaf Jah. Deccan was one of the most important areas in the Mughal Empire. The secession removed about one-third of the empire's revenue. It also massively thinned out its military strength. The Persian ruler Nadir Shah recognized the favor of the hour, moved in with his troops and defeated the Mughal army in the Battle of Karmal in 1739. The Mogul, hopelessly outnumbered militarily, granted Nadir peaceful entry into Delhi. There, widespread looting by the Persians took place. Among other things, the royal treasure was looted. Among them were the famous Koh-i-Noor and Darya-ye Noor diamonds, which are now part of the British and Iranian crown jewels, respectively. There were also bloody massacres of the civilian population. This and the high financial losses sealed the fate of the already weakening Mughal Empire. More and more provinces of the once great empire became independent again. Muhammad's power was reduced to a minimum and his sphere of influence included only the ransacked Delhi and Agra. The Maratha, on the other hand, expanded their sphere of power and the border of the Maratha Empire was extended to the Indus River. In 1748, Muhammad was able to repel an attempted attack by Afghan soldiers, but died a short time later. His successors were considered insignificant and weak and posed no obstacle to the invading Afghans, and so they conquered Sindh, Punjab and Gujarat. In 1757, Delhi was again ransacked. In addition to the Persians, the remnants of the empire were increasingly threatened by the Marathas.

EXCURSUS: THE BRITISH EAST INDIA COMPANY

The establishment of the British colony of India was largely driven by the British East India Company. This was a merchant company and joint stock company founded in London in 1600, whose primary goal was to intensify trade in goods from India. The establishment of such a trading company was not limited to Great Britain. Other European states also maintained corresponding East India companies. However, hardly any other company was granted such power in the following period. The East India Company of Great Britain was granted the right by the royal house to wage war, raise fortresses, administer justice and mint coins. Instead of being limited to trade, the company operated exactly as its name suggests: A Company in the service of the British Crown.

Over time, the East India Company developed into a state within a state. This was because its influence in England was growing. The wealthiest members of the East India Company were only too happy to be elected to parliament in order to strengthen their influence in the mother country as well. This was not difficult: the nouveau riche secured their votes by buying land. If such a person owned practically an entire voting district, the inhabitants automatically elected the landowner. This generated a dependence of the state on the members of the company. After all, they were not only the guardians over one of the most important colonies of all, but also interfered in politics back home. There were few dissenting voices from established politics. The company was the largest enterprise of the time. Thus, the state supported the company with further funding and new privileges.

In 1772, India's last great mogul, Shah Alam II, was forced to accept the British as a protecting power after being severely weakened. He was allowed to retain his symbolic title as ruler. However, his power was henceforth limited to his own palace, the Red Fort of Delhi. Delhi itself was under British control from the beginning of the 19th century.

It took some time for the British to secure such power. While trade interests, initially limited to Bengal, were still a significant motivation for the East India Company in the mid-18th century, the British quickly began to interfere with Indian rivalries. As early as 1757, the first major military confrontation occurred between the British and Indian princes. In 1771, Warren Hastings became governor of Bengal, which was in fact already part of the British Empire, and he massively accelerated the land takeover by concluding numerous so-called treaties of protection. Step by step, the British annexed vast tracts of land. The internal unrest in India emboldened the British: At any given time, there was always a party willing to cooperate with the British. This enabled a further expansion of the British sphere of power. Through this policy of expansion and alliance, some members of the East India Company managed to accumulate enormous wealth. This was because both the British employees and the Indian princes were corrupt to the core. This was one of the reasons why the East India Company itself got into massive trouble. Those in charge found it increasingly difficult to manage the ever-growing and entangled "colonial empire". Expansion cost vast amounts of money, which had to be provided by the company's shareholders. This did not work as expected and the East India Company accumulated a huge mountain of debt. For these reasons, the company was transformed in small steps into an administrative organization directly under the control of the British

Crown. The trading company effectively became a colonizing company. By 1834, this transformation was complete.

However, this reorganization did not mean that order prevailed in British India. The colonial rulers succeeded only inadequately in administering their territories. Particularly in the area of jurisprudence, there was complete lack of uniformity. The peculiarities of Islamic justice - especially the penal system, which was initially retained because of its simplicity - were difficult to reconcile with the British understanding of the law. Only the most cruel punishments, such as mutilation, were abolished by the British. In fact, there was no uniform criminal law at all until the 1860s. This lack of uniformity was further complicated by a confusing and sometimes useless bureaucracy.

There were differences in mentality between the former employees of the trading company and the officials now appointed by the British crown. While the merchants understood the purpose of acquiring language and regional ways of life, for example, in order to be able to negotiate more successfully with the natives, the higher officials saw themselves more as missionaries and colonial masters. The natives had to adapt to Christian ways of thinking and subjugate themselves to the characteristics of British or European culture.

When James Broun-Ramsay, a member of the British aristocracy, became governor general of India in 1848, the chaotic conditions were eliminated. Broun-Ramsay organized a rigid administrative system. The Indian princes were also subject to the British crown. This was especially evident when he introduced the Doctrine of Lapse, a simple but effective principle for the British occupiers to generate more influence. This doctrine stated that any state of an Indian prince would come under British control if the ruler had died without producing an heir. The peculiarity was that, according to the Doctrine of Lapse, an heir had to come directly from the bloodline of the prince. This was contrary to the traditional right of the prince to designate and thus adopt an heir to the throne himself, should he have no direct descendants. In short, if a prince died childless, his state went to the British Empire. But this was only one of the ways in which the British could appropriate further land. According to the Doctrine of Lapse, it was also possible to deprive a prince of his power if he proved to be manifestly incompetent. Exactly what this incompetence had to look like for the doctrine to apply was a matter of interpretation. The Doctrine of Lapse was perceived as an injustice by Indian nobles. However, there were initially no more than protests. Using those two tricks, Broun-Ramsay succeeded in annexing more princely states - the British colonial empire in India grew rapidly. The British plan had worked. Social reforms also fueled popular resentment. The inmates of prisons were no longer separated by the British according to their respective castes. This would have been unthinkable under an Indian ruler. Land reforms led to expropriation, excessive taxes and poverty. Over time, protests against the abolition of ancestral traditions turned into real anger, which expressed itself in resistance movements against the British colonial rulers and culminated in uprisings.

In the Sepoy Uprising, or more commonly called the Indian Uprising, Indians rebelled against the British. The movement got its name from the sepoys, Indian soldiers in the service of Great Britain. On May 10, 1857, troops first revolted against their commanders in Meerut. Subsequently, the revolt spread throughout the Ganges Valley and into central India. Cruel massacres took place. Sepoys as well as parts of the civilian population murdered British and other Europeans as well as Indians who had converted to Christianity. This in turn was interpreted by the British as a declaration of war, and a retaliatory campaign followed. The situation was aggravated by the Kanpur (former "Cawnpore") massacre. Indian troops had several dozen women and children slain with axes and hatchets. Shocked by this cruelty, the British responded with military ferocity, and it was successful. By 1858, the uprising had been largely quelled.

EXCURSUS: THE CARTRIDGES OF THE ENFIELD RIFLE

There is widespread scholarly consensus about the trigger of the Sepoy Uprising. The trigger was the increasing oppression and disenfranchisement of the native population by the British. The proverbial straw that broke the camel's back may have been the introduction of the British Enfield rifle to the sepoys. Its ammunition consisted of paper cartridges that were greased. The lubricant was either beef tallow or pig tallow. Before loading the rifles, the cartridges had to be bitten open with the teeth. The contact of Indian soldiers with these substances, all of whom were Hindus and Muslims, was a violation of their respective religious teachings for both faiths.

Many people died in the battles of the Sepoy Uprising. On the British side, about 2,500 soldiers are believed to have fallen; the Indian death toll exceeded these numbers many times over.

The sepoys' revolt had consequences. The British East India Company was finally dissolved and India became a crown colony of the Empire. The British public's reaction to the uprising was massive. This was because the public image of the subcontinent had been romanticized. Before the revolt, India was seen as a dreamlike fairyland full of riches and its inhabitants as oddball but peace-loving and deeply religious people. The fact that Indians were ready for violence shocked the British. As a result, the people of India, and especially the sepoys, were portrayed in the British press as murderous and bloodthirsty monsters. This further widened the gap between the two countries. In Great Britain, too, there were critical voices toward the country's own policies.

As an immediate reaction to the events, the British tried to strengthen their ties with the Indian noble houses. From then on, the occupiers wanted to refrain from undermining the ancestral traditions. Nevertheless, the last Mughal emperor was deposed in 1858. It was this formal act which finally eliminated the Mughal Empire, after which the last emperors had at most symbolic functions.

THE BRITISH INDIA COLONY

After the Sepoy Rebellion in 1858, not only did the Mughal Empire end, but so did the powers of the East India Company. The Government Act of India 1858 settled the Company's legacy. All the territories of the East India Company were officially placed under the British Crown. The administration of the colony was carried out by an institution called India Office from London. All the assets of the Company also went to the Crown. To add power to the implementation of the Government Act, the then Queen Victoria took the title of "Empress of India". This was because the East India Company had previously been subject to the Mughal emperors, at least in theory, although the members of the trading company were de facto the most powerful force in the country. By accepting the title of emperor, it no longer had its own administration. From a British point of view, this created the legal basis of the country's government. Two-thirds of the empire so created was administered directly by the crown. In the remaining third, regional princes took over administrative business under the direct control of the governor general, for whom the title "Viceroy of India" was created; governors became "Chief

Commissioners". The natives regained various rights that had been denied by the East India Company. Princely titles could again be inherited by adoption. Likewise, Indians and British were theoretically equal in their professions. Both populations could become civil servants. In reality, this modern reform looked somewhat different. Indians were usually denied higher positions in the administration. In general, this also offered many more career opportunities for the natives than before. By 1860, the map of India resembled a patchwork quilt. Great Britain's power did not cover the whole territory, but was interspersed by a large number of "native states".

Under the British, there was an economic boom during this period, although India was hardly industrialized. Rather, the British pursued the approach of growing raw materials in India, shipping them to Great Britain and manufacturing the corresponding end products there, which were then brought back to the Indian market on a smaller scale. As a result, India not only became a supplier of raw materials, but also a sales outlet. Important raw materials were jute, tea and wheat.

The infrastructure was significantly upgraded. Roads, canals, railroads and universities were built. Due to the fact that India continued to be agricultural, the majority of the population - usually simple farmers - hardly benefited from this upswing. First and foremost, only the British benefited from the improvement in the general situation. Only with a time lag did the positive effects of modernization reach the Indian population. Nevertheless, this was decisive for the further course of history, since a modern infrastructure favored the development of an Indian middle class. Some of the technologies brought by the British were readily adapted by the Indians, such as the book press. For the occupying British, maintaining the Indian colony was a costly endeavor. Maintaining the large army cost a lot of money. This was especially noticeable after the suppression of the Sepoy Rebellion, as the British saw an army composed entirely of sepoy as a potential nucleus of renewed resistance. Therefore, the composition of the Indian army was changed: In the future, every third soldier had to be European. This increased the expenses enormously, because the European soldiers were entitled to three times the pay. Another disadvantage was that Great Britain increasingly relied on India for support in conflicts.

Indians were fighting for the Empire all over the world. However, all of these expenses were declared as costs of the Indian colony, not Britain. As a result, the colony was deep in the red because of the enormous military expenditures. In 1909, military spending accounted for nearly 52 percent of the Indian budget.

Small revenues were generated from trade. The income from the levying of a land tax was far higher. Other taxes followed, for example for the use of forest areas and grazing lands. Traditional Indian tribes then rose up in revolt. Eventually, they were deprived of part of their livelihood. The resulting uprisings were usually put down by force. In addition to familiar tax formats such as the sales tax and income tax, the British established micro-taxes such as the salt levy, which was charged on the import of table salt. The revenue for the colonial rulers was negligible, but the effect was huge. The salt tax affected families as much as merchants, for salt was more than a spice in India. The most important staple food, rice, was prepared in salt water. The mineral was also used to compensate for the loss of electrolytes caused by hot temperatures. The lack of salt, or rather its price, fueled anger, and thus the salt tax became one of the engines of independence movements.

A significant break occurred in 1885, when the Indian National Congress (INC) was founded. The significance of the congress was initially manageable. Co-governance was not possible. Instead, members of the Congress could make requests and petitions to the British administration. Congress members were elite figures in Indian society. Their values and education were considered European. Even though the INC at this point was shaped according to the ideas of the British, it was to become the nucleus of the independence movement in the years that followed. The first step toward escalation took place in 1909. Since power in the INC rested predominantly with members of Hindu faith, the Muslim members split off and formed the Muslim League. Even though the League was basically in competition with the INC, in 1916 the two parties declared in writing a common goal: Indian independence. This event occurred in the midst of World War 1, from which India was not unaffected. About 1.3 million Indians fought on the side of the British. The idea of an independent India continued to mature. The most famous leader of the Indian National

Congress, Mahatma Gandhi, was instrumental in this process. Gandhi was a charismatic orator and perfectly understood how to convince the masses of his form of non-violent resistance to British rule. One of his stated goals was the unification of Hindus and Muslims in a united state. Like no speaker before him, Gandhi understood how to interweave the subjects of politics and religion. Thus his rallies had the effect of spiritual ceremonies. In 1919, there were mass demonstrations throughout the country. The discontent was triggered by various measures taken by the British. One of these was the Rowlatt Act, which allowed the colonial rulers to continue to apply special laws introduced during the war even in peace. These included, among other things, allowing people who were classified as terrorists to be arrested and held without a trial. Likewise, the arrest of (alleged) resisters was possible without further ado. An additional nuisance resulted from the deployment of Indian soldiers in the World War, who served primarily in the Middle East. According to general opinion, these veterans were not sufficiently honored by the British.

EXCURSUS: THE LIFE OF MAHATMA GANDHI

Mahatma Gandhi is probably the most important person in the history of India. Mohandas Karamchand Gandhi saw the light of day on October 2, 1869 in Porbandar, a small town in western Gujarat. His parents were wealthy, and his father was a senior minister. The Gandhis belonged to the caste of Vaishyas - merchants - and were therefore part of the upper class. He studied law in London from 1888 and was already fascinated by the idea of non-violent resistance. In 1891 he graduated, then settled as a lawyer in Bombay and Rajkot. He then moved to South Africa to work as a lawyer. At the same time, he campaigned for the Indian minority there and their rights. Gandhi founded a newspaper there, which contained texts in English and Indian. In South Africa, his political activism brought him into conflict with the law. Prison sentences followed. It was not until 1914 that he returned to India and began his non-violent struggle against the British colonial power.

By the way: "Mahatma" is not a first name, but an honorary title, which roughly means "With a great soul".

Even though Gandhi propagated nonviolent resistance, things did not always remain peaceful. For example, the Amritsar massacre in the city of the same name and the site of an initially peaceful demonstration against the British rulers escalated. The specific target was a protest against two local leaders of Indian nationalists. Relatively quickly, the situation escalated. Indian demonstrators set fire to administrative buildings and bank buildings as well as private homes. The region's governor, Michael O'Dwyer, responded by declaring martial law, and British soldiers moved into Amritsar. And even more, he explicitly ordered demonstrators to be fired upon. This led to a disaster. Several thousand people, who were demonstrating peacefully, gathered in a park that was surrounded by walls and had an exit in only one direction. This was blocked by about 150 British soldiers. In accordance with the governor's orders, they opened fire. The result was about 380 demonstrators killed and over 1000 injured. The commander of the troops, Brigadier General Reginald

Dryer, reported after the massacre that the demonstrators were armed revolutionaries.

Despite the horror of the Amritsar massacre, Gandhi and his followers were not dissuaded from the path of peaceful protest. Instead, they increasingly relied on civil disobedience as a means of protest. Gandhi called on his countrymen to stop working wherever they worked for the British. Administrations and factories were closed, railroad operations were also shut down, and Gandhi called for a boycott against all goods manufactured in Britain and distributed in India. The initial success was such that Gandhi thought he was already on the road to independence. Subsequently, the measures were tightened. Taxes were no longer paid and political elections boycotted. Gandhi always emphasized that any action should be taken only by peaceful means. He appealed to his followers to accept imprisonment without resistance. During arrests, the use of truncheons by the British police was common. Enduring this pain without striking back became a core element of nonviolent resistance.

Another central point of Gandhi's ideology was the unity of Hindus and Muslims. Thoughts like these were well received by many sections of India's population, but not everyone shared his attitude. In particular, Gandhi's idea of disobedience drew criticism from senior politicians and militant freedom fighters. The Muslim League in particular criticized Gandhi massively.

However, the success of the measures could no longer be denied. The British reacted quite helplessly to the mass strike, which affected all areas of life. Almost every Indian who responded to the call for disobedience joined Gandhi's Congress Party. The political base of peaceful resistance grew steadily. By now, the movement had swept the entire country. In the meantime, the empire was in shock. The government was almost completely undermined, and a lack of personnel meant that there was no longer a functioning executive branch. There were not even enough policemen, because even the law enforcement officers had defected to the side of the protesters. As a result, the British army had to take over police duties in the country. The situation slowly but steadily came to a head. Thousands of Gandhi's supporters were injured and killed. Thus, larger and larger parts of the movement moved away from the idea of peaceful protest. At first, British products such as textiles were burned on large pyres. At the end of this development, there were violent confrontations, the intensity of which increased steadily. At first, only unorganized individual actions were perpetrated on institutions and buildings. However, an outbreak of violence in the village of Chauri Chaura gained particular notoriety. There, a police station was set on fire and 15 policemen - Indians in the service of the British - were killed.

At this point, at the latest, Gandhi considered his peaceful coup to have failed and feared a further escalation of violence. Under no circumstances did he want to risk having formerly protesting people roaming the streets as a raging and killing mob. As a result, he officially declared the resistance against the British to be over. He blamed himself for the failure. He had insufficiently pre-warned his supporters about the importance of peaceful protest. This by no means had an immediate effect. Even though many of his supporters also condemned the incident in Chauri Chara, the resistance was not to be abandoned. The killing of the policemen was considered an isolated incident by many of Gandhi's followers. The "official" appeal to end efforts for independence was barely accepted by the protesters. It was only when Gandhi went on a hunger strike to emphasize his demand that millions of his followers were persuaded to give up resistance after fasting for three weeks.

He willingly allowed himself to be arrested immediately after the end of the resistance by the British, who sentenced him to six years in prison for publishing seditious writings. Gandhi's poor health - he had appendicitis - led to his early release from prison. Thus, the prison sentence ended after only 2 years and Gandhi was able to undergo a vital operation.

Mahatma Gandhi was still the leader of the Indian National Congress at this time. However, he was discouraged by the failure of his revolution. He was also losing power within his party. Although he was still able to rally many supporters behind him, oppositional currents were gaining strength within the National Congress. The Swaraj Party was founded, whose supporters were hostile to Gandhi as leader. Other Congress members, in turn, criticized the cessation of resistance due to the outbreaks of violence. Gandhi should not have allowed himself to be influenced by individual actions.

Nevertheless, Gandhi's theses on peaceful subversion had manifested themselves in the minds of the population, and he himself did not turn away from this philosophy. His following remained large, and Gandhi launched renewed campaigns of nonviolent resistance. Individual actions brought success this time, such as the Salt March. On March 12, 1930, Gandhi and about 80 of his followers marched from his home in Sabarmati Ashram to Dandi, which lies on the Arabian Sea. On foot, they covered 385 kilometers in 24 days. The aim of this action was to protest against the salt trade, which the British had completely under their control. There, on the coast, another action of civil disobedience followed. Instead of buying salt from the British at a high cost, the mineral itself was extracted. Bowls of seawater were placed in the sun. When the water evaporated, only salt remained. When the news about this action spread in India, many Indians followed the call. The British reacted sensitively, after all, the trade and extraction of salt was reserved only for them. It was considered a particular affront that the Indians not only used their own salt, but resold it. The salt monopoly was broken. As a result, the British had 50,000 Indians and almost all members of Congress arrested. The arrests accelerated the action and fueled the idea of resistance. Even though the Salt March was regarded around the world as a much-publicized example of peaceful resistance, little changed at first. Nevertheless, a central parliament composed of Indian politicians was to be created under the Government Act of India of 1935. This goal was a bicameral system consisting of an upper house and the "Federal Assembly", consisting of elected members. By extending the right to vote, 30 million people could now cast their ballots in elections (previously: 6.5 million). However, the establishment of a parliament could not be achieved. For both chambers, not enough Indian politicians or princes could be found who were willing to participate. A quorum was never reached. As a result, the central parliament remained at the 1919 level.

Elections were held at the provincial level, in which the Congress Party, also synonymous with Congress itself, largely prevailed as the strongest political force. Regions bordering other states were still excluded from self-government. That self-government promised greater autonomy for Indian provinces in theory, but it could be suspended at any time by the governor and placed under his direct control. Although this planned reform of the right of Indian politicians to have a say seemed modern, it was never actually implemented. This was particularly evident at the outbreak of World War II. The British people's rejection of the Nazis was explicitly welcomed by the broad mass of India's population. But even to enter the war, the significant majority of Indian politicians wanted to do so only if India itself gained independence. The then governor, Lord Linlithgow, ignored this proposal and legally declared war on Germany without consulting Indian politicians. This illustrated the de facto powerlessness of the National Congress. As a consequence, renewed demands for independence grew louder, but were again rejected by the British rulers. As a result, uprisings broke out, which were put down by force.

An important personality at this time was Subash Chandra Bose, Mahatma Gandhi's successor as president of the National Congress and his staunch opponent. He rejected the idea of peaceful overthrow and wanted to force the country's independence by military force. Furthermore, Bose was convinced that India's sovereignty could only be brought about with foreign policy support. In the 1930s, he traveled across

Europe for this reason and held talks with Benito Mussolini, among others. Shortly after the uprisings were settled following the British-Indian declaration of war on Germany in 1939, Bose was imprisoned as president of the National Congress. In prison, he went on a long hunger strike, and the British converted the prison sentence to house arrest - the fear of Bose's supporters reacting if he were to die was too great. In 1941, Bose finally made a spectacular escape via Kabul, Moscow, and finally the German Reich. His search for foreign support made at least partial progress. In mid-1942, he presented his request to German Foreign Minister Joachim von Ribbentrop and Adolf Hitler. The Nazi leadership was not convinced by his plans to support the Indians' struggle for independence: It was suggested he present his call for help to the Japanese Empire, which was allied with Germany. The Japanese were geographically closer to India and had fought successful battles against European colonial powers. Nevertheless, Bose managed to convince Hitler to raise a volunteer regiment to fight first alongside the German armed forces and later for India's independence.

EXCURSUS: THE FREE INDIA LEGION

Bose's legion consisted largely of Indians who fought for the British in North Africa and became German prisoners of war. Civilians in Germany also joined the regiment. The soldiers' task was initially "missionary": The volunteers were to convince other Indians in captivity to fight alongside the Germans for a "just cause", namely the liberation of India. In late 1942, the Free India Legion was deployed to the Netherlands and eventually transferred to the Atlantic Wall in France. There, the Indian infantrymen were also inspected by Field Marshal Erwin Rommel. Impressive photographs exist of this event. After the successful Allied landing in Normandy, the Legion was transferred to Germany and then back to France. During the retreat towards Germany, the Legion suffered its first losses. While attempting to make their way to neutral Switzerland, the Indians were captured by Allied troops and became prisoners of war. They were charged in Delhi: They were considered high traitors. Nevertheless, all the convicted members were released in 1946 after massive protests by the population. The troop strength of the Free

India Legion was about 2600 men and was subordinated to the Waffen SS. A special feature was their equipment: The Indians did not wear a steel helmet with their Wehrmacht uniform, but a traditional turban.

Following Hitler's advice, Bose set out for Madagascar on a German submarine and transferred there to a Japanese submarine. From there he was taken to Singapore, which was occupied by Japanese soldiers. Bose's reception was warm. With the support of the Japanese, he founded the "Indian Army" in Singapore, which consisted of about 40,000 Indian exiles and prisoners of war. In October 1943, he founded the Indian government-in-exile Azad Hind (in English "Free India"). The government was recognized only by the Axis powers around Germany, Italy and Japan.

In 1943, there was a great famine in Bengal. With the help of the Japanese, Bose offered to send rice to the British government in India for the starving population. The British turned down the offer. As a result, about two million people died of starvation. The Japanese themselves showed little interest in the Indian subcontinent. The empire was preoccupied with its own defeats in the struggle against the United States. The end of the empire was also the end of Azad Hind. After the dropping of atomic bombs on Hiroshima and Nagasaki, the Japanese and the troops of the Indian government-in-exile surrendered at the same time.

THE INDEPENDENCE OF INDIA

In August 1945, Bose wanted to fly to Tokyo from Singapore. His plane crashed and Bose was killed. His contribution to independence, which succeeded in 1947, was tremendous, but the means Bose used are still controversial today. Nevertheless, statues honoring Bose have been erected throughout India, especially in Bengal, where he is revered as a hero. For a long time, the Indian government wanted the legacy of Bose to be more or less hushed up. In general, he was hardly mentioned in public.

Even after the end of the Second World War, India did not come to rest. There were massive clashes between Hindus and Muslims. The positions of the opposing camps, the Indian National Congress and the Muslim League, came to a head. The British were able to put down uprisings only with the use of massive armed force and great effort. The problems on the British side were omnipresent and, surprisingly, negotiations on a possible independence of India actually took place. Mahatma Gandhi participated in those negotiations on behalf of the Indian National Congress, as did his successor Jawaharlal Nehru. Mohammed Ali Jinnah, the leader of the Muslim League, also took his place at the table. Plans for the country's future diverged. While Gandhi envisioned a united India, Jinnah pushed for a division of the country into a Muslim and a Hindu part - today's Pakistan and India. A fierce dispute broke out over this question, which spread throughout the country and once again led to violent clashes. This time, the British could not control the uprisings and wanted to get rid of the permanently unstable colony of India as quickly as possible. The original plan on the part of the British was to give India independence in 1948. In view of the uprisings, this step was brought forward and already a year earlier, in 1947, there were hasty power negotiations, initiated by the then governor Louis Mountbatten. The British governor of the colony of India was responsible for initiating independence. On June 3, 1947, he drew up a master plan to regulate the future administration of the country. India and Pakistan became independent and self-governing states and colonies (dominions), respectively. It was a plan that both the National Congress and the Muslim League could live with. The new borders were drawn according to religious majorities in the respective regions. Predominantly Muslim areas became part of Pakistan. Where Hindus formed the majority, modern India emerged. Mountbatten acted quickly. On August 15, 1947, state power was handed over and the borders redrawn - less than three months after the plan was drawn up. It was perfectly clear to most contemporaries that there was no alternative to this two-state solution. The rifts between Muslims and Hindus were too deep. Mountbatten was not criticized for this point. However, he was severely attacked for his tight timetable, which seemed to many observers to be absolutely rushed. And those were to be proved right: The new borders between the two countries quickly led to massive conflicts.

EXCURSUS: THE BORDERLINES OF CYRIL JOHN RADCLIFFE

The task of drawing up the new boundaries between India and Pakistan was entrusted to the lawyer Cyril John Radcliffe. Radcliffe himself was rather caught off guard by Mountbatten's tight schedule and faced the challenge of working under massive time pressure. In short order, he locked himself in his study to work out the boundary delineation and isolated himself from the outside world under the tightest security measures. Radcliffe's elaborations were presented to the public only one day before the independence of both states. From then on, the catastrophe took its course, as the border demarcation took no account of many important local realities. Thus, citizens who saw themselves as original Indians became Pakistanis overnight, and they felt that they belonged to the wrong state. Radcliffe's ill-considered works subsequently led to many wars, disasters and many millions of deaths. However, many historians agree that it was not Cyril John Radcliffe who was to blame for this debacle. Rather, it was Mountbatten who came under criticism. After all, he had given Radcliffe hardly any time to carefully work out what was already an extremely difficult task. When Radcliffe realized the implications of his plan, he broke with Mountbatten and waived his fee for the work on the India-Pakistan borderline.

After the announcement of the new borders following the partition of India, there were mass exoduses. Indians who considered themselves citizens of Pakistan fled to the new neighboring country and vice versa. Violence again broke out. During these migrations, more than a million people died. Among the dead was Mahatma Gandhi, who was shot by a religious fanatic on January 30, 1948. The problem: With the proclamation of the sovereignty of India and Pakistan on August 15, 1948, all principalities became independent, however small they were. The principalities joined either one or the other country. Almost all principalities chose sides by August 17, and by 1949 this process was complete. Only Hyderabad and Kashmir refused to join. In Hyderabad, the prince there initially tried to continue ruling independently - at least that was how it was supposed to look to the outside world. In reality, the ruler quietly established contacts with Pakistan, although the vast majority of the population were Hindus. Surprisingly, in September 1948, Indian troops occupied Hyderabad, which was now incorporated into India by force. In terms of denominational distribution, the reverse played out in Kashmir. After the new border demarcations were announced, violence escalated there. Insurgents under Pakistani command wanted to force the annexation of Kashmir to their country, as while most of Kashmir's population was of the Muslim faith, Kashmir was headed by a Hindu prince. The eventual annexation was welcomed by broad segments of the population there, who subsequently joined the insurgents. The Hindu prince's soldiers were unable to deal with the attack. In this example, after the mass exodus, another catastrophic flaw of the Mountbatten plan was revealed. After the bloody uprisings, the Hindu prince called for help from the newly formed India, which also claimed Kashmir. The violence escalated, and less than three months after independence, the first major conflict between the successor states of India and Pakistan occurred: the first Kashmir War.

The insurgents' successes multiplied, and on October 24, 1948, the state of "Free Kashmir" was proclaimed. India's intervention had its price. The Hindu prince had to assure them that after a successful suppression of the uprising, Kashmir would become part of India. The ruler accepted the offer and Indian troops moved in on October 27. Initially, the capital Srinagar was occupied by Indian soldiers. After initial successes, the Indian campaign stalled, particularly due to supply problems. Pro-Pakistani troops rallied and reorganized. A stable front emerged and significant Indian land gains failed to materialize. Nevertheless, it is worth noting that no regular troops from the state of Pakistan had been involved in the conflict until this point. Pakistan supported efforts to annex Kashmir until then. This did not make a real difference in the course of the war: Indian troops maintained the upper hand, but there was no "winner" of the war. The United Nations brokered an armistice between the two countries, which went into effect on January 1, 1949. This included a partition of Kashmir. Two-thirds of the territory fell to India, with the rest going to Pakistan. In addition, the UN drew a so-called ceasefire line, which still has the status of a de facto border. However, it is not recognized by either Pakistan or India. Around 8,000 people lost their lives in this first major conflict between the two states.

THE REPUBLIC OF INDIA

Even though the British granted independence to their former colony in 1947, India lacked a constitution. The Republic of India was not proclaimed until November 29, 1949, and the first constitution came into force on January 26, 1950. Rajendra Prasad, a member of the National Congress and party of the same name, became president. Initially, Prasad was to administer this office as interim president, but he was confirmed as president in the first presidential election in 1952 with 83.8 percent of the parliamentary votes. Prasad served as the country's president until 1962. His tenure was marked by efforts to establish a better education system. Gandhi's former comrade-in-arms, Jawaharlal Nehru, became the country’s first prime minister. The first parliamentary elections were held between October 1951 and February 1952. The Congress Party became the strongest force, securing three-quarters of the seats in parliament. In the 1950s, the last remnants of colonial rule disappeared, yet India remained a member of the Commonwealth. The French and Portuguese also still had bases in India at this time, which were gradually vacated. While the French left the country more or less voluntarily, the Portuguese were expelled with military force and their outposts, such as Goa, were annexed. Domestically, reforms were sought and new federal states were formed. In foreign policy, India maintained close contact with the Soviet Union. A planned economy was installed based on the Soviet model, and Prime Minister Nehru promoted industrialization. In terms of a market economy, the country pursued a course of isolation. High tariffs led to the greatest possible isolation from the world market.

In 1959, tensions grew with China, India's neighbor to the north and east. At the beginning of independence, relations between the two states were quite friendly. However, the relationship between the two states became more and more strained due to border disputes. The British, in consultation with Tibet, had previously drawn the border between China and the then colony of India, the so-called McMahon Line. The line runs across the Himalayas from Bhutan to the bend of the Brahmaputra River in the east. China did not accept this demarcation. Additional tension arose when India granted asylum to the Dalai Lama, who was persecuted in China, and he founded a Tibetan government-in-exile on Indian territory.

The heated situation escalated and the Indo-China Border War began. Without a declaration of war, Chinese soldiers crossed the McMahon Line in the northern and eastern parts of India on October 20, 1962. The Indian troops focused on the attack in the north and were completely surprised by the invasion in the east. A counterattack was hardly possible. Assured of victory, China declared a cease-fire on November 21. India did not comment on it, but also let the weapons rest. This was tantamount to India's defeat, even though there was little change in the border demarcation between the two states after the war. 2,000 people lost their lives in this conflict. The conflict between China and India - despite some rapprochements, such as talks on borders and trade agreements - continues to smolder today. As recently as June 2020, there were clashes on the border in which 20 Indian soldiers lost their lives.

In 1962, a new president was elected, Sarvepalli Radhakrishnan. Radhakrishnan is considered an important philosopher and pioneer of neo-Hinduism. Prime Minister Nehru died in 1964, and he was succeeded by Lal Bahadur Shastri, who was also a longtime comrade-in-arms of Mahatma Gandhi in the struggle for independence. In August 1965, the Second Indo-Pakistani War broke out. Once again, the issue was Kashmir, a problem that had been simmering constantly between the two parties since the first war in 1947. Pakistan saw itself as superior to India. The country had rearmed militarily in previous years and was supported with arms shipments from the United States. During the war, both parties were supplied with U.S.-made weapons. An additional weakening of India was suspected due to its defeat in the war with China. From Pakistan's point of view, the time seemed favorable to integrate Kashmir, which at that time was an Indian state under the name Jammu and Kashmir, into its own territory. The actual war was preceded by border conflicts in the Rann of Kachchh, a marshy area on the southern border of India and Pakistan. Although oil deposits were suspected in the approximately 28,000 square kilometer area, which is practically uninhabited, it was considered economically unimportant. Initially, there were individual firefights between border troops, which escalated into a massive conflict beginning in April 1965. Pakistan retained the upper hand in this local small-scale war. Under British mediation, a cease-fire was set for July 1. The borders were also minimally drawn. 900 square kilometers of the originally Indian part of the Rann of Kachchh were awarded to Pakistan. For the Pakistani side, this was considered a bad deal, as 3500 square kilometers were originally claimed. However, this regional conflict was considered a sideshow. The conflict in Kashmir itself was initially fueled without the use of official troops. Pakistan smuggled insurgents into the state of Jammu and Kashmir to incite the Muslim population there to revolt. The first violent clashes between insurgents and Indian police forces occurred in early August. Since the revolt was clearly organized by Pakistan from the Indian side, Indian troops set in motion and crossed the cease-fire line (effectively the border) to occupy the Pakistani part of Kashmir. This remained the only success of Indian troops in the area. Due to a massive underestimation of Pakistani military power, India suffered the heaviest losses. Massive strategic errors in reconnaissance also contributed to this defeat. Entire artillery units of the Pakistani army were simply overlooked. The war spread to Punjab a month later. In response to Pakistan's military successes in Kashmir, Indian troops crossed the India-Pakistan border in a large-scale offensive. The objective was to occupy the agriculturally important Punjab plains. More important, however, was the offensive on Lahore, still Pakistan's second-largest city by population. Pakistan sought international assistance and found it in the United States and China, which in turn now threatened India with war. Both countries maintained friendly relations with Pakistan. A real threat came from China in particular, while the United States had little interest in further escalation. Involvement of China would have extended the conflict throughout the region and unimagined consequences for the population would have been the result. With the support of the United States and the Soviet Union, the United Nations sought to resolve the conflict. Meanwhile, fighting continued. On September 16, the Battle of Chawinda occurred, lasting nearly a week and representing the largest tank battle since World War II. About 200 tanks were used on both sides and the losses were massive. Generally, it came down to a draw. Although Pakistan was technically superior, the Indians were able to make up for this disadvantage with their troop strength Meanwhile, a possible entry into the war by the People's Republic of China became increasingly likely, and the UN Security Council urged a cease-fire, which both parties to the conflict accepted. Peace was restored to Kashmir on September 23. Nothing had changed in the demarcation of the border as a result of the Second Indo-Pakistani War: Territorial gains were annulled at a conference moderated by the Soviet Union, and Kashmir was no exception. The territory continued to be claimed by both sides and the pre-war borders were restored - so the conflict was not resolved. After all, peace prevailed for the time being and the troops of both parties had been completely withdrawn by February 1966. The prime minister Lal Bahadur Shastri had already died the previous month, and he was succeeded by Indira Gandhi, the daughter of Jawaharlal Nehru. The similarity in name to Mahatma Gandhi is purely coincidental; there were no family ties. The prime minister was not free of criticism. In particular, she clashed with the old elites within the Congress Party. The reasons for these conflicts were, in particular, the nationalization of India's major banks and the cancellation of the pension payments of former princes. The tension within the party was so tense that a split was inevitable. The larger part of the Congress Party stood united behind Indira Gandhi, the smaller part since then operated under the name Congress O, (The "O" stands for "organization" and later became part of the newly founded Janata Party). The breakaway wing of the party posed no threat to Gandhi. In the 1971 parliamentary election, she won an overwhelming majority of the votes. Indira Gandhi's term of office included the Third Indo-Pakistani War. The dispute was initially based on a domestic political conflict in Pakistan. When elections were held in East Pakistan (east of India) in 1970 and 1971, the so-called Awami League won a major victory there - much to the annoyance of the military regime that ruled in the western part of the country, which was also west of India and saw its power threatened by the strengthening of the opposition league. In short, the military regime did not accept the election results, which further fueled efforts to achieve independence. West Pakistani forces were able to arrest one Awami League leader, but the rest of the leadership fled into exile in India and proclaimed independence for the Pakistani province of Bangladesh. Independence of the province was considerably in India's interest. This was because the country lay between West Pakistan and East Pakistan, and in the event of war it was therefore able to avoid a war on two fronts.

At the same time, the people of West Pakistan were suffering the consequences of a devastating cyclone that hit the country hard in November 1970. Up to half a million people were killed. As a result of the emerging Bangladesh conflict, India closed its borders with western Pakistan. Relief supplies stopped arriving. This led to mass migration, and the flow of refugees from western Pakistan to India swelled to 10 million people. In East Pakistan, India became involved in training guerrilla fighters and sent its own paramilitaries into the country to support the separatists. This resulted in a significant intensification of the conflict. Pakistan responded in early December with a massive air strike and bombardment of facilities on Indian territory. The conflict was also fought at sea; an Indian warship was sunk by a submarine. On December 16, the war in East Pakistan ended when West Pakistani forces surrendered. In West Pakistan, the war ended a day later. As a direct result, Pakistan's military government resigned and Bangladesh became independent. The conflict thus resettled the power structures in the region. Nevertheless, the Third Indo-Pakistani War does not remain in the consciousness because of the military actions. During the conflict, Pakistani soldiers committed atrocious crimes against Bangladeshi civilians in East Pakistan, including mass executions and mass rapes. Historians estimate that approximately 200,000 women were abused. In total, there is talk of up to 3 million deaths. Bodies were still being discovered in mass graves decades later.

There was no peace even after the ceasefire. In 1974, India started its nuclear program and detonated its first atomic bomb underground, which again led to tensions between the neighbors.

EXCURSUS: OPERATION SMILING BUDDHA

The first test of an Indian-made nuclear bomb took place on May 18, 1974, and was camouflaged as Smiling Buddha. The name and timing were precisely chosen. The operation fell on the day of the Vesak festival, the highest Buddhist holiday. The bomb was detonated underground in Rajasthan and had the explosive power of 8 kilotons of TNT: Pakistan reacted angrily to the test. Pakistani leaders viewed the test as a threatening gesture. A scheduled meeting on the future peaceful future of the two countries was summarily cancelled. Historians are certain that the detonation of the first Indian atomic bomb massively accelerated the development of a Pakistani bomb. Thus, a regional nuclear arms race including the characteristics of a cold war emerged.

Despite this demonstration of power to the outside world, the period that followed was marked by massive internal unrest and strife. The mood within the population was bad, and social reforms were demanded. Riots broke out everywhere, prompting Indira Gandhi to declare a state of national emergency in 1975. This state of affairs meant a serious curtailment of the population's basic democratic rights, and the prime minister ruled the country as dictator for almost two years. Democratic elections were to be held in March 1977, which confirmed the prime minister in office. However, the ruling Congress Party achieved a disastrous election result and was replaced by the relatively new Janata Party, which henceforth formed the government. This situation did not last long. Internal strife caused the government to fall apart, and new elections were held as early as January 1980. In the early elections, the Congress Party once again prevailed: Indira Gandhi became prime minister again.

In Punjab, the Sikhs, a religious minority, revolted on July 19, 1982. The goal of the insurgents was to declare a state of their own. The situation was difficult for the prime minister to handle. In June 1984, an order with symbolic power was issued. Gandhi had soldiers storm the Golden Temple in Amritsar, the highest shrine of Sikhism. Sikh rebels were suspected in the temple complex. For Indira Gandhi, this act had fatal consequences. Sikhs were also in her service as bodyguards. Two of the bodyguards turned on her after storming the temple - Indira Gandhi was killed by them on October 31, 1984. This in turn caused a storm of indignation among Gandhi's followers. There were riots against Sikhs everywhere.

Indira's son, Rajiv Gandhi, was nominated by leading Congress Party politicians to succeed her as prime minister. In the December 1984 general election, the Congress Party won an overwhelming victory and Gandhi became the new prime minister. Abroad, the new prime minister, who was considered a liberal politician and an excellent diplomat, was quite popular. He held talks with Pakistan to stabilize peace in the region and established closer ties with the People's Republic of China. During his reign, the Indian army was deployed on various missions abroad, for example in the Maldives and Sri Lanka. Rajiv Gandhi was not too popular among his own people. He was considered erratic, fickle and someone who did not stand by his own promises. In addition, there were massive accusations of corruption, and scandals surrounding Rajiv made the rounds. He was physically assaulted at events during his election campaign in 1987. A security guard struck Rajiv with the butt of his rifle, but the prime minister survived unharmed. In 1991, he was assassinated near the city of Madras by a female suicide bomber, a member of the LTTE, a paramilitary organization that pursued the goal of achieving an independent Sri Lanka. A total of 18 people died in the attack. By that time, Rajiv Gandhi was no longer prime minister. He had already lost the confidence of his electorate by a wide margin and was not confirmed in office in 1989, being replaced by Vishwanath Pratap Singh of the Janata Dal party, which had been founded shortly before. Singh was unable to establish a stable government. Early elections had to be held as early as 1991. The winner of the election was Pamulaparthi Venkata Narasimha Rao of the Congress Party, who took over the reins of government again, but with a minority government. Rao remained in power until 1996 and initiated various market-economy reforms. However, the country did not find peace. Conflicts flared up again in the state of Jammu and Kashmir, which had been in a state of emergency for years. Afghan radicals crossed the border into Kashmir and tried to incite the Muslim majority there against Hindus. The reverse occurred in India itself: Ultramilitant Hindus destroyed an important mosque in the city of Ayodhya in the state of Uttar Pradesh. Under these circumstances, the next election took place in 1996. There was no clear winner, and various governing coalitions took turns. Kocheril Raman Narayanan became president in 1997 and held the office until 2002. New government elections were held in 1998 and 1999. It was not until 1999 that a viable coalition of a number of different parties was established with Atal Bihari Vajpayee as prime minister. Vajpayee was a member of the BJP, the Bharatiya Janata Party, a right-wing conservative party. As a result, the conflict with neighboring Pakistan, which was always smoldering anyway, came to a head again. The subject of the renewed dispute was once again Kashmir.

The conflict is rarely referred to in the literature as the fourth Indo-Pakistani War, because no official declaration of war was made. Therefore, it is more often referred to as the Kargil War. In actual fact, at that time, there was an effort to finally resolve the Kashmir issue. The intention to settle the conflict was recorded by both parties in the Lahore Declaration. However, at the same time as the signing, armed Pakistanis crossed the cease-fire line, which was still in effect. This happened in the Kargil district in the north of the Indian state of Jammu and Kashmir. There, the Indian Army still maintains numerous positions over a distance of 160 kilometers, which it usually abandons in winter due to challenging climatic conditions. At that time, in January, these posts were unoccupied and consequently taken by armed men from Pakistan. These were not official troops at first, but by May, regular Pakistani soldiers had begun to move into Kargil. This was discovered by the Indian Army only at that point, in May. Reconnaissance teams counted up to 900 fighters, including those regular troops, but this was vehemently denied by the Pakistani government. The Pakistani military equipment that had now arrived in Kargil, however, testified to the involvement of regular soldiers. Special equipment for high mountains was brought in, as well as artillery, anti-aircraft guns and mortars. India responded with a rapid buildup of troops in the region by May 26. With Operation Vijay, the Indian military leadership launched the offensive on the ground and in the air. The latter proved virtually useless. The much better-equipped Pakistani troops shot down one fighter plane and one helicopter. The impassable terrain also meant that the Indians were hardly able to gain any ground. The Kargil mountain ranges gave Pakistani troops an excellent defensive position. Indian efforts focused on securing the highway from Leh to Srinagar. The highway was the deployment area for the Indian Army, but it was under heavy artillery fire there. Accordingly, the surrounding positions were to be eliminated first. This succeeded: the Pakistani troops were pushed back into the hinterland. The Indian military leadership deliberately refrained from pursuing their opponents. This would have resulted in the cease-fire line being crossed and consequently in open conflict. Slowly but steadily, the Indian troops gained the upper hand. The occupied positions in the Kargil were recaptured by India by July 1999. A special position in this conflict was held by former U.S. President Bill Clinton. In talks with Nawaz Sharif, the Pakistani prime minister, the latter announced that he would withdraw his troops from Kargil. There had never been an official acknowledgement of such deployment in the area up to then. This announcement was tantamount to an admission that troops were indeed present in Kargil, but Sharif only described the soldiers as “freedom fighters”, thereby distancing himself from their deployment. This "confession" did not result in further escalation, and hostilities ceased on July 14. India can be considered the victor in the Kargil conflict. Resolution of Kashmir’s status was still in the balance. After the conflict, the borders reverted to their pre-war status. Casualties amounted to about 5,000 men on the Pakistani side, while no more than 600 Indian soldiers fell. In Indian media, the outcome of the conflict was almost over-celebrated. Prime Minister Vajpayee gained in popularity in this patriotically charged atmosphere. In the long run, the Kargil conflict had the effect of bringing India closer to the United States. Pakistan, which triggered the conflict by occupying India's mountain positions, became more isolated from the international community. One exception was China, an important partner of Pakistan, which had massed its troops on the Sino-Indian border in the aftermath of the battle for Kargil. Basically, the prevailing opinion among the Indian public was that it was steadily maturing into a major regional power. To strengthen this claim, several tests of nuclear bombs were again carried out under Vajpayee. Unimpressed by this, the Pakistani government supported Muslim rebels in Kashmir. In 2002 and 2003, the countries were again on the verge of military escalation. At the same time, increasingly hostile sentiment toward Muslims was noted in India. In 2002, riots against Muslims living in Gujarat, a state in western India, were carried out by Hindu militants. The ruling Bharatiya Janata Party with Prime Minister Vajpayee came under criticism for being too timid in combating the violence. This brought massive criticism to the BJP, with moderate Hindus in particular criticizing the government. This may have been one reason why the BJP was unable to hold on to power in the long term. The then opposition Congress Party achieved the strongest result in the 2004 elections. The president of the Congress Party and widow of Rajiv Gandhi would have effectively been elected prime minister, but she relinquished the post. Instead, power was transferred to the Sikh Manmohan Singh. Since that time, India has been marked by an economic boom. The gross domestic product has grown by an average of 7.5 percent per year. Singh's declared goal was to raise the standard of living of the Indian population and to bring India closer to its arch-enemy Pakistan.

DIGRESSION: CRICKET DIPLOMACY

Apart from their British colonial past, the states of India and Pakistan do not have much in common. Religious differences and border disputes determine the relationship between the neighbors. But there is one passion that unites the citizens of both nations: Cricket. The somewhat lengthy game with bat and ball is a remnant of the colonial era and is still beloved. Pakistan and India each field very good national teams. Indian Prime Minister Singh took advantage of this common ground. When state visits took place, cricket matches were often organized as part of the visit. A shared passion was supposed to open the door for further talks of peaceful coexistence and take some pressure off the tense summit meetings. This worked: from 2005 onward, small rapprochements between the countries have been recorded.

Singh was re-elected in the 2009 elections. Even though Singh advanced the country in certain aspects, he was not spared criticism. Massive allegations of corruption flared up again and again, especially during his second term. In 2014 and at the age of 81, Singh retired from politics, clearing the way for Narendra Modi, politician of the Bharatiya Janata Party. Modi was no stranger to India's history. In 2002, he was head of government ("chief minister") of the state of Gujarat. That year, serious riots broke out there between Hindus and Muslims. Earlier, there was a fire on a train packed with Hindu pilgrims. Whether the fire was caused by an attack or an accident has not yet been adequately clarified. For militant Hindus, it was clear that it was a terrorist attack carried out by Muslims ready to use violence. In revenge, Hindus attacked Muslims indiscriminately, and there were rapes and pogroms. Some 2,000 people met their deaths. The chief minister apparently reacted little to these atrocities. This earned him criticism. The U.S. saw Modi as a major culprit for the numerous deaths and barred him from entering the country. Modi was also heavily criticized in India itself. In 2009, the Indian Supreme Court looked into the massacre and found no evidence to prove Modi's complicity. Arson was determined to be the official cause of the train crash. His attitude toward people of the Muslim faith is widely viewed as controversial to this day. The subject of criticism is a 2019 decision by Modi that allowed refugees from the Middle East or Pakistan to become naturalized citizens in India. This applied to Hindus, Christians, Sikhs, Buddhists and others, but explicitly not to Muslims, which resulted in massive protests by Indian Muslims.

Although the country has been spared wars in recent years, it has suffered all the more from natural disasters. The tsunami triggered by a seaquake with an epicenter in the Indian Ocean on December 26, 2004, claimed the lives of between 12,700 and 16,000 people, depending on the source. In 2019, the country had to contend with a severe heat wave.

As prime minister, Modi is pursuing the goal of making the country more economically fit. In order to make India a more attractive location for foreign investors, tax cuts have been made. Administrative structures have been reformed to keep bureaucratic hurdles to a minimum. An important topic on Modi's agenda is digitization. Budgets for other areas, on the other hand, were cut massively, especially in environmental protection and healthcare. The level of pensions has also been reduced. Since Modi took office, a deterioration in relations with Pakistan has been evident. The Indian prime minister has repeatedly accused the Pakistani government of being a supporter of Islamic terror. Further rapprochement, on the other hand, took place with neighboring Bangladesh and with Israel. The state of Jammu and Kashmir was partitioned. Until then, the state had a special status, which was initially revoked until the territory was absorbed into the Union Territories of Jammu and Kashmir and Ladakh. When this step was taken on October 31, 2019, it hailed criticism from the Pakistani government, which for its part still harbors territorial claims to Kashmir.

- Chapter 2 -

THE REPUBLIC OF INDIA - OVERVIEW

With a population of 1.393 billion people (as of May 2020), India is the second most populous country in the world after the People's Republic of China with around 1.4 billion inhabitants. According to current projections, however, India will replace the Chinese as the most populous country in the coming years. At the same time, India is the most populous democracy. The area of India is 3,287,263 square kilometers making India the seventh largest country in the world. The national territory is framed by two natural borders: the Himalayas in the north and the Indian Ocean in the south. India's six neighbors are Bangladesh, Myanmar, Bhutan, Nepal, Tibet (Autonomous Region of the People's Republic of China) and Pakistan. Other neighbors that lie in the Indian Ocean are Sri Lanka and the Maldives. The longest border is shared with Bangladesh (4,053 kilometers), the shortest with Bhutan (605 kilometers). The total length of the borders is 14,103 kilometers. The extent of the country from north to south in the maximum is 3,200 kilometers, from west to east it is 3,000 kilometers. The Indian territory also includes various offshore island groups: The Laccadive, Amindivi, Andaman and Nicobar Islands and the island of Minicoy. The Kangchenjunga is the third highest mountain on earth at a height of 8,586 meters. It was considered the highest mountain until 1852. Numerous rivers flow through the country. Particularly important rivers are the Ganges, the Brahmaputra and the Indus, from where the name the name India is derived. Other important rivers are the Yamuna, the Gomti and the Chambal.

THE INDIAN POLITICAL SYSTEM

According to the constitution, India is a parliamentary democratic republic with a federal structure. The constitution was adopted on November 26, 1949, and entered into force on January 26, 1950. The constitution is divided into a preamble, a main body and a total of twelve annexes. The preamble assures citizens of the following ideals: social, political economic justice, freedom of expression, freedom of thought, freedom of belief and confession, and freedom of worship. Other important points are equal opportunities and (political) equality.

The catalog of fundamental rights reflects the state's self-image as sovereign, socialist, secular and democratic. The word socialist was added to the preamble in 1976 and underscores the state's claim to a sociopolitical orientation.

The preamble defines the fundamental rights of the Indian people and includes liberty rights, protection against exploitation, religious freedom, protection of minorities and the right to constitutional complaints. Since the adoption of the constitution, the preamble has been modified. For example, the subsection defining a right to property for Indian citizens was removed in 1978. To this day, the deletion causes controversial debates.

The catalog of fundamental rights as such refers in some parts to the British colonial era. Rights that were once reserved exclusively for the governors found their way into the constitution. Certain similarities to a presidential constitution can easily be seen. According to the British model, the prime minister bears the power to govern. The president's duties are primarily representative. His powers are limited, however, and he is not authorized to act without consulting the prime minister and the Council of Ministers. In its basic features, the Indian constitution is partially comparable to the French constitution.

The fundamental rights also enshrine general human rights, such as equality before the law and non-discrimination against people of other religions, genders, origins and races, as well as castes. Importantly, it abolishes the concept of so-called untouchability, a feature of the Indian caste system. Discrimination against members of the "untouchables" caste (see chapter "The Caste System in India") was made a punishable offense.

The powers in India are separated, consisting of a legislative, judicial and executive branch. The head of state and commander of the armed forces is the president, who also appoints the prime minister and, with his consent, the council of ministers. To be appointed prime minister, the candidate must be the leader of the party (or alliance of parties) that won an absolute majority in the lower house of parliament in the most recent elections. The prime minister-designate does not necessarily have to hold a seat in the lower house, but can also "only" be a member of India's upper house.

To aspire to the office of president, there are few formal hurdles that must be overcome. The President of India must be at least 35 years old and a citizen of India, and be eligible for re-election. The president is the chief representative of the executive branch. His deputy is the vice president, who, in the event of his death, takes over until a new president is elected. If there is a violation of the constitution, the president can be removed from office by a two-thirds majority. The actual head of government is the prime minister.

Constitutionally, the prime minister is subordinate to the president. In real terms, however, it is the prime minister who must make the most important political decisions. Although the constitution states that he must advise the president, de facto it is the prime minister who determines political decisions.

The Prime Minister is the chairman of the Council of Ministers, the cabinet of the government. Ministers vary in rank: Cabinet ministers, who are responsible for heading a ministry; independent ministers of state, who do not oversee a specific area of responsibility; and ministers of state, who report to cabinet ministers and participate in their ministries. The prime minister himself does not usually take charge of a ministry, but is considered responsible for all ministries in their entirety. India has an extraordinarily high number of ministers. More than 80 ministers are possible, which corresponds to about 15 percent of the total seats in the lower house.

India's legislature, or lawmaking, is the Parliament, which is divided into two chambers: the Lok Sabha, the "House of the People“" the lower house, and the Rajya Sabha, the "House of the States" (also "Council of States"), the upper house. India's system of government is strongly reminiscent of Great Britain's parliamentary system. India's parliament building, Sansad Bhavan, is located in New Delhi.

The lower house is the first chamber of parliament and holds the most important decision-making power in India, especially when it comes to budgetary issues. In principle, the lower house is equal to the upper house. If there are different votes, the two bodies deliberate in a joint session. However, this only happens extremely rarely. The last time this happened was in 2002, when a new anti-terrorism law was to be passed that was discussed very controversially in public. A maximum of 550 seats can be allocated in the lower house; currently there are 545 seats. Two of these will be directly appointed by the president. These individuals are to represent the Anglo-Indian minority in the country. The chairman or speaker of the lower house is elected by the assembly. Parliamentarians must be at least 25 years old and Indian citizens. The official language is English, but Hindi is also used and simultaneously translated. In addition, the use of 22 other Indian languages is permitted. Exactly which languages these are, is regulated in the constitution. If a parliamentarian wishes to make a speech in one of these languages, this must be officially announced in advance within an individual deadline so that a translation into English and/or Hindi can take place. Depending on the language chosen, this notification period can be 30 minutes or even a whole day. The second chamber is the upper house, whose members are elected by the parliament of the states and some of the union territories. Not all territories are represented in the upper house. This is due to the fact that no assemblies are held at their regional level. The Upper House may have a maximum of 250 members. Twelve of them are appointed directly by the President. These special members usually possess "outstanding ability" in various sciences or arts. The remaining 233 parliamentarians are elected by the regional parliaments, as mentioned above. This is possible insofar as the potential representative has Indian citizenship and a minimum age of 30. They are elected for a legislative period of six years. The chairman of the upper house is the vice president. There has been a quota for women in both the lower and upper houses since 2010. Since then, one-third of the deputies in both chambers must be women.

In addition to the two houses, the president also has the right to legislate. This is done through the use of ordinances, which must, however, be submitted to Parliament. These ordinances can be objected to by Parliament. If this is not done, the ordinance automatically enters into force six weeks after submission and subsequently becomes valid.

The official language at the court is English, but switching to the regionally predominant language is possible at the lowest level of the jurisdiction.

EXCURSUS: THE 2001 ATTACK

In December 2001, relations between Pakistan and India reached a new low. The two states were on the verge of another military confrontation. The reason: On December 13, there was a terrorist attack on the parliament. Five attackers threw grenades at the parliament building and fired machine guns. 14 people died in the attack and 27 others were injured. The Indian government blamed Pakistan for this act of terror. In fact, the attackers were extremists from the Islamist organization Jaish-e Mohammed, which operates out of Pakistan. The perpetrators themselves were from Jammu and Kashmir. Four of the five perpetrators were arrested and sentenced to prison. The organizer of the attack was sentenced to death. The death sentence was carried out in February 2013.

The further division of powers in the states follows the same pattern as at the federal level. Each state is headed by a governor, who is appointed by the prime minister and heads the executive and legislative branches. At the state level, the governor appoints the members of the Council of Ministers and the chief minister, who has de facto decision-making power. The relationship between the governor and chief minister is similar to that between the president and prime minister. The governor and prime minister are the heads of government at the various levels. Here, too, the chief ministers actually have an advisory function, but "impose" their advice on the governor and compliance is taken for granted.

The states have a legislative system that is very similar to the national parliamentary system. However, these parliaments do not necessarily have to consist of two chambers. Therefore, there are states with a unicameral system. If the parliament has two chambers, these are divided into a lower and upper house and follow the national model. If there is only one chamber, it is called the Legislative Assembly. Whether the parliament is defined as unicameral or bicameral is up to the states. The vast majority of states use the unicameral system. The dominant form of parliament is therefore the Legislative Assembly, which can have up to 500 members who are elected directly by the people for a legislative period of five years. There is also a one-third quota of women in these bodies. In the case of concrete legislation, the governor is also able to introduce a law on his own authority as an ordinance. This procedure corresponds to the way things are done at the national level. If the compulsory approval of the assembly follows, the law becomes legally effective.

India has several levels of judiciary. The Supreme Court is the highest body of the Indian judiciary and is based in New Delhi. The presiding judge is the Chief Justice. The primary function of the Supreme Court is to settle disputes between the government and the states and other countries. Each state has its own supreme court and a total of 24 in number. This represents the second tier of Indian jurisdiction. However, such a court may have jurisdiction over several states. This also applies to the Union Territories. All of these courts are subordinate to the Federal Supreme Court and deal primarily with appellate cases. Criminal courts and civil courts operate at the third level. There are also separate criminal courts in the various districts.

ADMINISTRATIVE STRUCTURE

According to the constitution, India is a federal republic and consists of a total of 28 federal states and 8 union territories. While the states are self-governing, the territories are directly subordinate to the federal government.

The 28 states are (sorted by population, with capital city indicated, as of 2011):

- Uttar Pradesh (199,812,000, Lucknow)
- Maharashtra (112,372,000, Mumbai)
- Bihar (103,804,000, Patna)
- West Bengal (91,348,000, Calcutta)
- Madhya Pradesh (72,598,000, Bhopal)
- Tamil Nadu (72,139,000, Chennai)
- Rajasthan (68,621,000, Jaipur)
- Karnataka, (61,131,000, Bangalore)
- Gujarat (60,384,000, Gandhinagar)
- Andhra Pradesh (49,387,000, Amaravati)
- Odisha, (41,947,000, Bhubaneswar)
- Telangana (35,287,000, Hyderabad)
- Kerala (33,388,000, Thiruvananthapuram)
- Jharkhand (32,988,000, Ranchi)

- Assam (31,169,000, Dispur)
- Punjab (27,704,000, Chandigarh)[1]
- Chhattisgarh (25,540,000, Raipur)
- Haryana (25,353,000, Chandigarh)[1]
- Uttarakhand (10,117,000, Dehradun)
- Himachal Pradesh (6,865,000, Shimla)
- Tripura (3,671,000, Agartala)
- Meghalaya (2,964,000, Shillong)
- Manipur (2,722,000, Imphal)
- Nagaland, (1,981,000, Kohima)
- Goa (1,458,000, Panaji)
- Arunachal Pradesh (1,383,000, Itanagar)
- Mizoram (1,091,000, Aizawl)
- Sikkim (608,000, Gangtok)

The Union Territories of India are:

- Delhi, (16,788,000, New Delhi)
- Jammu and Kashmir (12,549,000, Srinagar and Jammu respectively)
- Puducherry (1,244,000, Puducherry)
- Chandigarh[1] (1,055,000, Chandigarh)

---

[1]The city of Chandigarh is the joint capital of the states of Punjab and Haryana, as well as the administrative seat of the Union Territory of Chandigarh itself. This unusual administrative

- Andaman and Nicobar Islands (380,000, Port Blair)
- Dadra and Nagar Haveli (343,000, Silvassa)
- Daman and Diu (243,000, Daman)
- Lakshadweep (64,000, Kavaratti)

Uttar Pradesh is the state with the most inhabitants. In terms of area, Uttar Pradesh ranks only fourth with an extension of 243,300 km². The states of Rajasthan (342,200 km²), Madhya Pradesh (308,400 km²) and Maharashtra (307,700 km²) have a larger area. The smallest state is Goa with an area of 3,700 km². The largest Union Territory in terms of area is the Andaman and Nicobar Islands (8,200 km²), and the smallest is Lakshadweep - also an island group - with a total area of only 32 km².

Larger cities with several hundred thousand inhabitants usually administer themselves through Municipal Corporations, while Municipalities are responsible for smaller cities. A special feature is the Panchayati Raj form of administration, which is used especially in rural areas.

---

structure is based on the disputed affiliation status as well as reforms of the Indian states.

EXCURSUS: EACH VILLAGE MANAGES ITSELF

The Panchayati Raj is a decentralized form of administration already advocated by Mahatma Gandhi. Basically, the premise is: Each village administers itself. Such an administrative unit is called Gram Swaraj and is divided into three levels: Village, Block (consisting of several villages) and District (consisting of several blocks). This principle of administration was introduced in various states as early as the 1950s and 1960s. An amendment to the Constitution, recorded in 1992, confirmed the principle, although the modern manifestation differs significantly from the original variant. However, the basic idea is still present. Taxes, among other things, are levied and collected at the village level, and the same applies to customs duties and other fees. Block administrations are responsible for medical care, drinking water supply and sewage disposal, operation of elementary school, road construction and its maintenance. At the district level, the respective administrations handle issues such as the operation and construction of hospitals, libraries, bridges and much more.

According to the 2011 census, there were 46 cities in India with a population of over one million people. The capital New Delhi in the state of Delhi is the second largest city in the country with 11 million inhabitants. Mumbai in the state of Maharashtra is India's largest metropolis and has a population of 12,478,000. Other major cities are:

- Bangalore (8,426,000 inhabitants, State: Karnataka)
- Hyderabad (6,810,000, Telangana)
- Ahmedabad (5,571,000, Gujarat)
- Madras (4,681,000, Tamil Nadu)
- Kolkata (4,487,000, West Bengal)
- Surat (4,462,000, Gujarat)
- Poona (3,115,000, Maharashtra)
- Jaipur (3,073,000, Rajasthan)

POLITICAL PARTIES IN INDIA

There are many different parties in India's political spectrum. A basic distinction is made between national parties and state parties, i.e., according to whether they are active nationwide or only in the states and their parliaments. There is no obligation for a party to register officially. However, such a step brings with it some privileges. For example, a party symbol. This can be a flower, an animal or an object. This symbol is provided by the Indian Election Commission and offers increased recognition among illiterate voters. In addition, registered parties have the right to broadcast election advertisements on radio and TV.

To register as a national party, at least six percent of the votes in the election to the lower house, the Lok Sabha, are required. Alternatively, six percent of the electoral votes in the elections to the parliaments in four states are sufficient. As another option, 11 delegates in the lower house from three states also suffice. These rules have only been in place since August 2016, because before that the entry requirements were considered too low. Until then, it was sufficient for a party to be recognized in at least four states in order to achieve national status. If this was the case, the party in question was automatically considered a national party.

To be recognized as a party in principle, the hurdles are also quite low. All that is needed is 100 supporters to confirm party status. Finally, the chairman - called party president or secretary general - must present the party program and pay a fee of 10,000 rupees. In addition, he must not have a criminal record. The party must be committed to the Indian constitution. To obtain state party status, similar regulations apply as for recognition of national party status.

Currently (as of 2019), there are eight Indian national parties.

- The Indian National Congress (INC), or Congress for short, was founded in 1885. Along with the Bharatiya Janata Party, it is considered India's people's party. It stands for a social democratic or socialist-democratic and secular worldview and has an estimated 20 million members. The INC has provided most of India's prime ministers and presidents. In the current lower house, the INC has 52 seats and is part of the opposition. The chairperson is Sonia Gandhi, and the party symbol is the outstretched hand.

- The second people's party in India is the Bharatiya Janata Party, or BJP. It has the most members of any party in the country (147.8 million). In 2015, the BJP was even the party with the most members worldwide. The BJP is considered to be decidedly conservative and at times authoritarian. It stands for national conservatism in general and Hindu nationalism in particular. It has formed the government since 2014 and has 303 seats in the lower house. The chairman is Amit Shah, and the party symbol is the lotus flower.
- Another national party is the AITC, the All India Trinamool Congress, which presents itself as primarily socialist, anti-communist and secular. In past elections, the AITC was able to take large parts of the electorate away from India's communist parties. In the current lower house, the AITC holds 22

seats, making it a party in broad opposition. Its chairperson is Mamata Banerjee, and its symbol is an undefined sprouting plant.

- The Bahujan Samaj Party (BSP) is another national party that plays an important role almost exclusively in the state of Uttar Pradesh. It belongs to the social-democratic camp and sees itself primarily as representing the interests of the casteless (Dalits). The chairwoman is simply called Mayawati. Her full name should be Mayawati Prabhu Das. The BSP has nine votes in the lower house. Its symbol is the elephant.
- The Communist Party of India, or CPI, is a communist or Marxist-Leninist party. According to its own information, the party was founded in 1925. Its general secretary is Doraisamy Raja. Despite its status as a national party, it plays a clearly subordinate role in Indian political life. It has two seats in the lower house. The party symbol consists of ears of corn and a sickle.

- The second communist party in India is the Communist Party of India (Marxist), abbreviated as CPM. It is a split from the CPI and was founded in 1964. Its general secretary is Sitaram Yechury. Like the larger CPI, its role is marginal and it holds three seats in the lower house. A sickle, ears of corn and a gavel form the CPM's party symbol.
- The Nationalist Congress Party (NCP) focuses on federalism, progressivism, nationalism and secularism and was founded in 1999. Its chairman is Sharad Pawar. The party won five seats in the last Lower House election. The NPC is an opposition party. Its symbol is the clock or an alarm clock.
- The National People's Party (NPP) sees itself as the political and democratic representative of India's indigenous peoples and was founded in 2013. Despite its status as a national party, the ethnocentric party operates predominantly at the regional level. The party's president is Conrad Sangma. The

NPP has one seat in the lower house of parliament, and its party symbol is a (closed) book.

The current lower house is composed of six factions in the current election period. The government is formed by the Bharatiya Janata Party (see above for orientation), the Shiv Sena Party (national-Hindu), the Shiromani Akali Dal (party of the Sikhs) and the Lok Janshakti Party (representing the lower castes/Dalits). The ruling parties have 329 seats in the lower house, the majority of which are held by Bharatiya Janata Party MPs (303 seats). The direct opposition is called the United Progressive Alliance (UPA) and is led by the Congress Party. Other member parties include its allied parties, most of which are on the moderate political (i.e., democratic) spectrum. The UPA has 61 seats in the lower house. The quite considerable number of remaining seats in the lower house, 143 in all, are classified as "other parties", a broadly diversified mass of the most varied political tendencies The CPI, the CPM and the Revolutionary Socialist Party form a kind of bloc with six seats. Two additional seats are allotted to the nominated politicians as representatives of the Anglo-Indian population.

A similar distribution of parties can be observed in the upper house, the Rajya Sabha. Here, too, the Bharatiya Janata Party dominates with 58 of the maximum 250 seats (note: some of the seats are vacant). The second strongest force is the National Congress with 54 seats. The remaining seats are shared by representatives of 26 other parties, independents and nominated members.

THE POPULATION OF INDIA

According to the authorities, India's population in May 2020 was 1.393 billion people, about 12 percent of the world's total population. The trend is upward. Even though the government is trying to curb the population explosion with birth control programs, India will overtake China as the world's most populous country by 2023 at the earliest and 2030 at the latest. In 2020, each Indian woman had an average of 2.24 children. By way of comparison, this figure was 5.90 in 1955. Due to the still high birth rate, there is a strong surplus of children and young people in India - every fifth child currently born worldwide is Indian. The median age is about 28 years. Infant mortality has been reduced through various medical programs and educational efforts. However, the death rate among children remains high. Between 2015 and 2020, about six million children under the age of five died.

In British colonial times, average life expectancy was still less than 30 years. Today, life expectancy is 70.4 years for women and 67.8 years for men, practically doubling over the last 70 years. Independence has played a major role in this: Living conditions have improved, as has access to better basic medical care. Despite this upward trend, life expectancy can vary in different regions, as not all states are equally developed. The standard of living in India is therefore not homogeneous.

EXCURSUS: MASSIVE SURPLUS OF MEN

In India, there is a high imbalance in gender distribution. An Indian peculiarity in the past was that girls had a lower life expectancy than boys. This was an almost unique demographic feature worldwide. In the meantime, however, this trend has normalized. Today, there are about 940 women for every 1,000 men. Extrapolated to the entire population of the country, this makes for a surplus of 65 million men. This fact is deemed as the cause of the continual increase in sexualized violence and rape.

The reasons why there are more men than women today can also be found in Indian history. Even in colonial times, girls were killed after birth in order to save bride money in the event of a later marriage. In general, boys were preferred in society, girls were considered inferior. Even today, girls are aborted more often than boys. To prevent this, the government banned the determination of a baby's sex by ultrasound examination. Human rights organizations complain that this ban is implemented only half-heartedly or not at all.

Poverty is a major issue in many parts of India. However, the economic upswing has significantly reduced the poverty rate. Whereas in 2005 around 55 percent of the population still lived in poverty, in 2015 the figure was only around 28 percent. The poverty rate has almost halved in this period. Today, about 3 percent of India's population lives in extreme poverty. This group has a daily income of less than $1.90. Even though poverty has been drastically reduced over the last 15 years, social misery is widespread. About 15 percent of Indians were considered undernourished, according to a 2019 United Nations report, up from about 22 percent in 2005. One manifestation of this is short stature; more than one-third of Indian children are too short for their age. The Indian population has the smallest average height in the world. Malnutrition is compounded by poor hygienic conditions. A program under the heading "Clean India" was adopted in 2014 and has since improved the situation. Child labor is a very big problem, especially in rural areas. Often their own children are the only available labor in the countryside. Many farmers still live in a form of debt bondage and often work off debts owed to the respective landowners. Their own income remains low and paying off debts is often not possible. It is believed that over 17,000 farmers have already taken their own lives due to the hopeless situation. As a result of these grievances, an increased rural exodus has become noticeable. However, only a few refugees succeed in improving their living conditions in the cities of India. There is a lack of work and housing. This has already led to the massive increase in the number of slums in the past, which continues to grow. In Mumbai, the largest slum in Asia exists with half a million inhabitants. On average, about 30 percent of all inhabitants live in such slums in shanty towns.

A major problem in increasing prosperity is the underfunding of state institutions such as schools or hospitals. Hospitals, for example, are available, but they are understaffed or not equipped with necessary technical equipment. Both technology and personnel are financed by tax money. However, these are chronically scarce, as only one percent of the population pays any taxes at all. At the end of the

2000s, government spending on the health care system was only 1.58 percent. The inadequate health care system and poor education are clearly reflected in the spread of HIV. Even though the infection rate has been declining since the 2010s, India ranks third after South Africa and Nigeria in a global comparison of countries with the most HIV infections. In 2008, about 0.29 percent of Indians were HIV-positive. Transmission predominantly takes place through unprotected, heterosexual sexual intercourse with prostitutes.

To reduce transmission, India urgently needs a functioning school system that educates about the health risks. Nine out of ten children attend elementary school, but they are extremely poorly equipped. In a global comparison, the Indian school system is considered one of the worst in the world. There are too few teachers, miserable equipment and very outdated teaching methods. School classes are overcrowded. Basically, the Indian school system is in urgent need of reform. In terms of literacy, progress has been made in recent decades, even if the level does not stand up to comparison with Western standards. A 2011 survey found that a quarter of the total population could neither read nor write. In the first survey after independence, only about 18 percent of Indians could read and write. Women today have a lower literacy rate than men. One-third of women are illiterate, compared with only one-fifth of men.

India also has to contend with other social problems, especially homelessness, unemployment, environmental pollution and a very pronounced gap between rich and poor. Most of India's nearly 500 million workers have neither social security nor pension entitlements. These people are often helpless in the face of economic fluctuations. If a loss of wages threatens, due to unemployment or illness, the workers and their families find themselves in a difficult situation that often threatens their very existence. Reserves and savings that could cushion these shortages in times of need are hardly common, and there is rarely even the possibility of building up such collateral. Women participate comparatively rarely in gainful employment, and the man is considered the breadwinner of the family. Social disparities vary among the individual states, as well as between urban and rural areas. The regions in the south, Tamil Nadu and Kerala, and in the north (Delhi) have comparatively progressive wage levels. The same applies to centrally located Maharashtra. Regions such as Uttar Pradesh, Bihar, Rajasthan, Madhya Pradesh and the states in northeastern India are considered backward.

India is both a country of immigration and emigration. Most of the slightly more than 5 million immigrants come from neighboring countries such as Bangladesh, Nepal and Sri Lanka. However, these are only the official figures. About 20 million foreigners are believed to be residing in the country illegally, mainly from Bangladesh. India ranks twelfth in a global comparison of states with the largest proportion of foreign residents.

Almost 18 million Indians live abroad. If the descendants of Indian immigrants are also included in these statistics, the number rises to around 31 million people. The British, who used cheap Indian labor in their colonies all over the world, played a significant role in this figure, especially after the abolition of slavery. To this day, there are many people of Indian descent in Africa and Asia, as well as the Caribbean. Today, many (male) Indians migrate to the Arab world and especially to the United Arab Emirates to earn money as guest workers. Often, wages are transferred to family in India for survival. Highly qualified Indians often migrate to Western countries such as the USA, Great Britain, Australia or to the countries of the European Union. This "brain drain", i.e., the departure of well-educated academics, has a significant impact on the Indian economy and society. Medical professionals in particular often leave their home country. This leads to a massive shortage of doctors in rural regions.

THE INDIAN CASTE SYSTEM

A distinctive feature within the Indian population is the caste system. A caste describes a hierarchical system for dividing social groups. To this day, belonging to a particular caste shapes the way people live together in India, even though the negative effects, such as social discrimination, are prohibited by law. In the original tradition of the caste system, which developed about 2000 years ago, many areas of daily life were regulated. Marriages were performed exclusively within one's own caste. In addition, membership in a caste had a great influence on the exercise of one's profession. This has changed little to this day. Meals were also taken together with members of one's own caste. A common meal with lower castes was perceived as "defilement" until modern times. Today the picture is different, but varies from region to region. In some states, segregation during public meals is still maintained, although not quite as strictly as it once was. A comparatively strict interpretation continues to be given to the ideals of casteism during weddings. Marriage within one's own caste is still common, although it is no longer obligatory. Those wishing to marry, however, continue to face great pressure in conservative circles. The motive to marry a person outside one's own caste and the denial of this wish by one's parents is a common theme within Indian culture, for example in Bollywood films. Since India's caste system has religious roots and is more of a guide to the distribution of social tasks, membership in a particular caste does not indicate the material wealth of that person. Membership in upper castes does not signal simultaneous membership in the upper class. Basically, the caste system has some parallels to the medieval feudal system and estate system. People are "born" into a certain caste; it is not possible to change.

There are four main traditional castes, the varnas. Each caste is assigned a traditional occupational task and a color. As mentioned, the original professions today differ from the traditional form, which is listed below. The first caste are the Brahmins (color: white, intellectuals, priests), the second are the Kshatriyas (color: red, high officials, "warriors", princes, rulers), the third are the Vaishyas (color: yellow, merchants, traders) and the Shudras (color: black, farmers, craftsmen, simple workers).

EXCURSUS: PRIEST AT THE HEARTH

Even though the traditional choice of profession has determined the career path for many centuries, the situation today is different. Only a few Brahmins actually practice the profession of priest. Neither the president nor the prime minister must necessarily come from the Kshatriya caste, and their members rarely become soldiers or officers. Real reasons have a much greater importance in their choice of job than their status at birth. For example, Brahmins disproportionately often work as cooks in restaurants. The reason: fundamental Hindus consider it "impure" when food is prepared by members of lower castes. If the dishes are prepared by members of the highest of all castes, the problem is solved. Resourceful restaurateurs can therefore also attract customers from the ranks of arch-conservative Hindus, for whom the caste system is still very relevant, to their restaurants.

The four main castes are strongly subdivided into so-called jatis, subclasses of the castes. In the broadest sense, the jatis resemble clans or extended families.

How many such jatis there are is disputed. Estimates range from several hundred to several thousand jatis. In social interaction, these sub-castes are very relevant, because they fulfill important tasks. Belonging to a jati is like having social insurance, especially in the slums of India's metropolises. Those seeking help receive food and shelter or a job from the representatives of their own jati. In case of illness, they take care of each other. Within these jatis, exact social norms prevail, obliging the respective members to help. In effect, these clans fulfill a task that the Indian social system can only inadequately fulfill. Basically, the Jatis are the practical interpretation of the Varnas so, it would be atypical to ask an Indian about his varna. In everyday life, these are not considered meaningful enough and often have a negative connotation.

Social advancement beyond one's own jati is generally considered difficult, but not impossible. Entire jatis have been known to ascend in the social structure. This can be achieved when a higher-ranking jati serves as a role model and their way of life is imitated by the others.

The jatis are in turn subdivided among themselves. These subdivisions are called subjatis and signify even closer family structures. In the case of marriages (and arranged marriages), this affiliation takes on special significance: Marriage is strictly avoided within a subjati, in order to prevent incest.

In addition to the caste system described above, there are those people who are considered "casteless". These are the so-called Dalits. The term is misleading in that Dalits do belong to a jati, but not to a varna. Dalits are also referred to as untouchables in the traditional Hindu context. This designation is and has been applied to other people outside the caste system, such as Muslims and Christians. The Dalits have been systematically oppressed for centuries. Even though the constitution of India strengthens the rights of the Dalits and they are also specifically supported, the untouchables are still the target of discrimination and ostracism in everyday life. Conservative Hindus are not allowed to touch these people; they are considered "impure" in the traditional sense. Adherents of a fundamental interpretation of the caste system even avoid "touching" the shadow of Dalits. In society, Dalits have been denied access to certain professions and educational institutions. To combat discrimination, the government has introduced Dalit quotas at universities.

RELIGION IN INDIA

The majority of the Indian population - almost 80 percent - belongs to the Hindu faith. The second most important religion in the country is Islam, with around 14 percent. About 2.3 percent of Indians are Christians, 1.7 percent Sikhs and 0.7 percent Buddhists. 1.3 percent of the population belong to other religious communities.

In principle, the various religions coexist comparatively peacefully, even though there have been regional conflicts with massive consequences in the past. The last major outbreak of violence was in Gujarat in 2002. (see History of India).

INDIA'S FOREIGN POLICY

Since their independence, India's foreign policy has been strongly dominated by its tense relationship with its western neighbor Pakistan. There have hardly been any tension-free periods: If the two powers are not in (armed) conflict with each other, they have almost always been on the verge of it. The trigger is always Kashmir, which is claimed by both sides. Nevertheless, the permanently smoldering conflict is not a small war between neighbors. Nuclear armament gives the India-Pakistan conflict a special significance. If a state arms itself with nuclear weapons, this is a clear signal to the entire community of states: A conflict with India is pointless. Since independence, the country has increasingly seen itself as a major regional power. The subcontinent as such, including Kashmir and large parts of the Indian Ocean, is regarded as India's sphere of interest. The western world takes much less notice of this conflict than it does with other, non-western states. Russia, for instance, clearly stakes its claim on the countries of the former Soviet Union and is willing to use force to achieve it, as was the case with Crimea. Actions like these inevitably attract the attention of the international community. In the case of India, the rise to regional power has been more subtle, with the exception of the Kashmir conflict But India's interests do not stop in Kashmir. A visible sign of India's rise is its permanent seat on the United Nations Security Council, in addition to its nuclear armament. Nevertheless, India is seen as a state where precise guiding principles sometimes seem difficult to pinpoint. After independence and the breakaway from Great Britain, the Indian government avoided taking sides in the emerging East-West conflict. Initially, India became part of the non-aligned states and took the leading role there. In foreign policy, the new India presented itself as emphatically peaceful and cited the peaceful coexistence of all peoples as its ideal goal. Neutrality on the part of the West and East made it possible for India to give priority to its own domestic and foreign affairs. Nevertheless, India has slowly been distancing itself from the West and its idealism leans toward the Soviet Union. One sign of this was the orientation of the economy, which exhibited planned-economy characteristics. The fact that the United States supported its arch-enemy Pakistan with weapons further distanced India from the West. India subsequently had to contend with a loss of international prestige. A turning point was India's abstention from the UN's condemnation of the Soviet Union after its invasion of Afghanistan in 1979. India had an interest in an Afghanistan that was hostile to Pakistan. India drew further criticism for its dealings with smaller states in its neighborhood. India increasingly acted as a great power and bullied its neighbors. One example was the Indira Doctrine of 1983, which obliged neighboring states to seek India's help only if internal conflicts arose. Other states were not to be allowed to interfere, causing the self-determination of neighboring sovereign states to be undermined.

In terms of foreign policy, India found itself in an increasingly isolated position in the late 1980s. In the Soviet Union, the urge to reconcile with China prevailed instead of supporting India, which was also a rival of Beijing. The United States, on the other hand, lost interest in Pakistan as a strategic ally after East-West relations increasingly relaxed. The end of the Cold War further reduced the importance of the non-aligned States. However, the general pacification of the global security situation contrasted with India's future path, for nuclear armament continued to be the focus here, and the Nuclear Non-Proliferation Treaty was not ratified by India. The goal behind this was obvious: India wanted more prestige in the world and to pave the way to becoming a great power. This certainly caused irritation in the international community. After India's atomic bomb tests, the U.S. reacted with economic sanctions, although a rapprochement between the two nations was actually underway.

After the terrorist attacks in New York in 2001 and the resulting war on terror, India announced that it would henceforth refrain from testing nuclear weapons and would not proliferate nuclear weapons any further. A nuclear first strike with a nuclear weapon was categorically ruled out by India. This was a move with diplomatic foresight: skillfully, India profiled itself as a "Mighty Power that responsibly renounces its power". This self-portrayal remarkably improved India's status in the world. Former U.S. President George W. Bush first publicly referred to India as a great power in March 2006. The two countries concluded a nuclear agreement, and for the first time in more than 30 years, the United States sold radioactive material to India for civilian use. However, India did not turn away from its own nuclear program.

Nevertheless, relations between India and the USA improved considerably. The Indian economy was liberalized and the country became a major trading partner of the USA. Numerous American companies increasingly invested in India as a business location. The Indian-origin population in the USA is quite large and many Indian students spend study visits there. The USA is a popular emigration destination, especially for highly qualified professionals.

Relations with Russia have also improved in recent years. Compared with the Soviet era, however, the relationship cannot be described as particularly friendly. A historical problem burdened relations until the 1990s: India had accumulated enormous debts to the Soviet Union, which could now be repaid by India on quite positive terms. Initially, India's nuclear weapons program was a burden that caused irritation and skepticism in Russia. Nevertheless, treaties of friendship and a so-called "strategic partnership" were concluded in the meantime, and armaments cooperation was intensified.

India's relationship with China has also been easing since the mid-1990s. For decades, the People's Republic had been a significant rival in India's power spectrum. An important basis for the improvement in relations was the agreement ratified in 1993 to defuse the conflict on the Sino-Indian border, which was reaffirmed in 1996. A final solution to the border disputes is unlikely to be found in the foreseeable future.

China's far-reaching cooperation with Pakistan, especially in arms matters, created uncertainty. In addition, the Chinese installed missile sites in Tibet and a naval base as well as listening posts in Myanmar. India responded by intensifying relations with Vietnam. Despite what should be improved relations, India and China remain major competitors in the greater Indian Ocean region. Within India's sphere of power aspiration, China remains the greatest threat. This is also the reason why nuclear disarmament is currently out of the question for India. The possible threat from the People's Republic is explicitly mentioned in such questions. Beijing reacts to India's nuclear tests with the greatest protest. This is because China also regards India as a major competitor in South Asia. Through nuclear armament, India has been able to expand its position of power, much to China's displeasure. Beijing has repeatedly expressed negative views about India's seat on the UN Security Council and disapproves of India's bilateral relations with the United States. There is concern that the U.S. is building a strong ally in its immediate neighborhood. Accordingly, the Chinese government supports India's fiercest rival, Pakistan, in arms matters. Nonetheless, the countries are converging somewhat; the volume of trade between the two states is growing. Moreover, Beijing has moved to condemn India's foreign policy actions on principle simply because they come from India. For a long time, China supported Pakistan's position on the Kashmir issue because they are competitors of India. China's leadership has since moved away from this.

In the entire South Asian region, India acts as the dominant great power vis-à-vis its smaller neighbors. From India’s point of view, this behavior is explicitly acceptable. Its legitimacy is based on its possession of nuclear weapons, its comparatively superior (conventional) military power, its economic performance and its large population. The geographic factor also plays a role: India has the largest land mass in southern Asia. As a result, relations with neighbors are very close, but not necessarily cordial. If there are disagreements with neighboring states in the area of foreign policy, India often reacts quite harshly and refers to its regional superiority. The Kingdom of Bhutan is practically a satellite state of India, and their relationship with Nepal is similarly close. These ties were made possible by a large number of trade agreements and protective treaties. In the case of Nepal, India is the military protector, which is particularly important because of its proximity to China and the autonomous region of Tibet. With Bangladesh, the Indian government initially maintained extraordinarily cordial contacts. After all, the northeastern state was once Pakistani territory, and India was instrumental in them gaining their independence. Gradually, conflicts arose, triggered, for example, by the massive movement of refugees from Bangladesh to India. Another vexing issue has been unclear border demarcations. One serious problem was the construction of the Farakka Barrage by Bangladesh, which was completed in 1969 and 1970. The barrage diverted some of the water from the Ganges River, which was desperately needed by Indian farmers to irrigate their fields. Only a treaty regulating the distribution of the Ganges water was able to solve this problem.

India has also emerged as a regional power. This became clear in the case of the civil war in Sri Lanka from 1983 to 2009. India intervened militarily in 1987. Their justification for this was the close relations between the inhabitants of Sri Lanka and the inhabitants of the Indian state of Tamil Nadu. The regional government there independently threatened military intervention in the civil war. The Sri Lankan government, however, requested military assistance from the United States and Israel. India, as a self-declared protecting power, considered this unacceptable. As a result, India arbitrarily sent a peacekeeping force and exerted political pressure on Sri Lanka. Neither was crowned with success: The fighting could not be ended by Indian troops. At the request of the Sri Lankan government, the Indian soldiers withdrew. This represented a considerable loss of prestige for India. Public opinion was that the limits of India's capabilities as a protective power had been reached.

There are cordial relations with Germany. After the founding of the Federal Republic of Germany, the Republic of India was one of the first states to recognize the Federal Republic diplomatically. Close relations prevail especially in the area of trade. Within the European Union, Germany is India's most important trading partner, a major advisor on economic issues and provides development aid. Particularly important here, for example, is the "Agenda for Indo-German Partnership in the 21st Century", a declaration adopted in May 2000 that set the framework for an intensive partnership. Several focal points, such as energy efficiency and environmental protection, dominate the dialogue. In addition, economic projects such as the establishment of Indian companies are supported.

- Chapter 3 -

THE INDIAN ECONOMY

The Indian economy is growing steadily and efficiently. According to an estimate of the International Monetary Fund, the gross domestic product (GDP) amounted to 2,256 billion US dollars in 2019. Thus, in terms of the amount of GDP, India occupies the fifth position in the international comparison behind the United States, China, Japan and Germany. India was able to generate a higher GDP than leading industrialized nations such as Great Britain, Russia or France. In the same year, the economy grew by 4.04 percent, compared with 6.1 percent for its competitor China.

By definition, India's economy is a managed planned economy. Consequently, the influence on the market is great. In particular, the domestic market was heavily regulated by the government in the decades before 1990. This was intended to protect the domestic market from competition from abroad, but resulted in lower economic growth than is the case today. Since the 1990s, the influence of the state has been reduced more and more. After Chandra Shekhar's reign, a reorientation of the economy began. Structural deficits were seen as an obstacle, so the government began to liberalize the economy and turn away from a strictly planned economy. In 1992, a five-year plan was passed under Prime Minister P. V. Narasimha Rao. One hurdle that had to be overcome initially was the impact of a previous economic crisis. India had run up massive debts in previous years. To deal with this problem, for example, subsidy programs were stopped and government spending drastically reduced. In addition, foreign trade was reformed and gradually opened to the world market. Customs duties and tariffs for importing goods were lowered. The export ratio also increased by about 20 percent due to a devaluation of the Indian rupee. There was a departure from the managed regulation of the domestic market. Increasingly, private entrepreneurs were allowed to gain access to economic sectors that had previously been entirely state-owned, such as banking and finance. For the first time, investors were also allowed to take out foreign loans, and bureaucratic hurdles to starting a business were lowered. Agriculture initially remained unaffected by the reforms. Step by step, manufacturing companies in this sector were also rapidly privatized. Within the five-year plan from 1992 to 1997, economic growth of 5.4 to 8.0 percent per year was achieved. In 1991, growth was only 1.4 percent.

A key initiator of economic reforms was Manmohan Singh, who held the office of prime minister from 2004 to 2014. The government still had to contend with a high budget deficit, which in some cases amounted to up to ten percent of GDP, for example in 2009/2010. Nevertheless, the economy grew under Singh, especially the industrial sector and the service industry. And yet India remains an agricultural country. About two-thirds of all workers earn their money in the agricultural sector, an industry where efficiency is subject to strong fluctuations due to the monsoon.

THE INDIAN RUPEE

The Indian rupee is a currency with a long tradition. Its introduction dates back to 1526, when the currency was still called rupya and was a silver coin. In 1612, the coin was given the name rupee. The first banknotes were introduced in the 18th century. In 1825, the British pound became the nationwide currency in India, but it did not really catch on. The rupee remained the number one means of payment at all times.

A major problem in India was (and still is) the mass hoarding of cash in private households. This was one of the reasons why Prime Minister Narendra Modi felt compelled to withdraw all 500 and 1,000 rupee bills in November 2016. Within 50 days, the population had the opportunity to exchange these old bills for new ones. If this did not happen, the old bills would become ineffective and thus worthless. The fight against corruption and money laundering was also put forward as an argument. The cash exchange ended in disaster. ATMs and banks could not be supplied with the new bills in time. In short, cash became a scarce commodity. Long lines formed in front of banks, and sometimes people had to wait several hours for cash. The situation appeared anarchic: 70 people died in the queues. As a result, economic growth fell by one percent, and the government was accused of a failure across the board. As a consequence, the director of the central bank resigned.

At that time, over 700 million Indians had no bank account. The reform of the banknotes hit the rural population particularly hard: The bills were used to pay day laborers and there was no possibility of exchanging them, especially in the countryside. Thus, workers were paid with banknotes that would soon become worthless. The workers did not want to accept this and, as a result, work was suspended and the fields were no longer cultivated. To cope with the currency crisis, foreign countries rushed to help. The then U.S. President Barack Obama supported the Indian government within the framework of the "strategic partnership". As part of this partnership, it was agreed to work together in the field of nuclear energy and the foundations were laid for deeper economic cooperation.

The Indian rupee is also a common means of payment in other countries, including especially the small neighboring states of Bhutan and Nepal. The exchange rate in June 2021 was approximately one euro to 88 rupees.

INDIA'S AGRICULTURE

About two-thirds of employed Indians work in the agricultural sector. Most of them are small farmers or self-suppliers. According to the World Bank, most Indians live in small villages, of which there are just under 650,000 spread across the country. This equates to about 860 million people living and subsisting off of agriculture. As mentioned, adverse weather conditions in large parts of India make farmers' work very difficult. While water is abundant during monsoon seasons, crops wither during prolonged dry spells. As early as the 1960s, the government responded to this challenge. Farmers increasingly switched to fast-growing cereals and rice in particular. Today, India is the world's second largest rice producer after China. In total, nearly 25 percent of global rice production comes from India. Other important crops include oilseeds, pulses, potatoes and various fruits. Important export crops include coffee, tea, jute, rapeseed, peanuts, sugar cane, cotton and spices. Livestock breeding has been neglected. Slaughter cattle are hardly being produced. On the other hand, there is a large market for dairy products. Even though gigantic quantities of agricultural products have been produced at times, productivity has been low and, by global standards, backward and hardly competitive. Products are not being processed adequately. For example, United Nations observers estimated that 40 percent of crops become inedible due to a lack of refrigeration capacity and packaging materials.

EXCURSUS: THE IMPORTANCE OF THE COW IN INDIA

The cow is a sacred animal in Hinduism. This is partly because deities often take the form of a cow. This is how they are depicted in the myths. In addition, the god Krishna is said to have grown up with cowherds. The mother of all cows named Kamadhenu is also important in the faith. Basically, cows are sacred and therefore untouchable. And whoever kills a cow is considered a murderer. After all, cows give the "Five Holy Gifts", namely butter, milk, yogurt, dung and urine. This means that a cow may also be used for commercial purposes. Dairy products are popular and the industry is very significant for the Indian economy.

It is different with the meat. Beef is not allowed as food among Hindus. Traditionally, the owner has to care for and feed the animal until the end of its life. In practice, the situation is different. Often the cows are sold to Muslims and slaughtered at an advanced age, i.e. when they no longer give milk. Dalits are also not subject to this food taboo. As a result of their beliefs, many Hindus live completely vegetarian.

In 2020, a comprehensive reform was carried out under the slogan "One India, One agricultural market". In view of the volatile agricultural sector, the reform was urgently needed and had the effect of liberalizing the agricultural market. This resulted in a further move away from the original planned economy. Farmers can now choose more individually which crops they want to grow and to whom they want to sell them. Farmers can conclude contracts directly with exporters and wholesalers. Indian agriculture is, and was, in dire need of reform, a fact which became evident in view of the competition present within the industrial and service sectors. In 2019, the agricultural sector accounted for only 16 percent of GDP. This is at odds with farm employment figures. In 1991, agriculture accounted for 27 percent of GDP, according to the World Bank.

INDIA'S FOREIGN TRADE

India has a foreign trade deficit. In 2020, goods worth 368 billion U.S. dollars were imported and goods worth 276 billion U.S. dollars were exported. This means a deficit of 92 billion U.S. dollars. However, this deficit is falling steadily. In 2018, the balance was still -185 billion U.S. dollars; in 2019, it was -155 billion U.S. dollars. Among imported goods, petroleum is by far the largest item, accounting for 17.5 percent of total imports. Other important goods include chemical products (14.6 percent), electronics (10.6 percent), machinery and machinery parts (7.3 percent), gold (6 percent), nonmetallic minerals (5.2 percent), coal (4.5 percent), gas (4.1 percent), and electrical equipment (3.4 percent).

Important export goods are: Chemical products (19.2 percent of India's total foreign trade), food products (11.3 percent), textiles or apparel (10.2 percent), petrochemical products (9.5 percent), nonmetallic minerals (7.4 percent), machinery and machinery parts (7.2 percent), iron and steel (4.6 percent), motor vehicles and motor vehicle parts (4.5 percent), and electrical equipment (2.6 percent).

By far the most important import partner is China. 16 percent of all imported goods come from the People's Republic. Other important importing countries are the USA (7.2 percent of all imports), the United Arab Emirates (6.5 percent), Saudi Arabia (4.8 percent), Iraq (4.4 percent), Hong Kong (4.0 percent, considered separately from China because it is a Chinese special administrative zone) and Singapore (3.3 percent). The top buyer of Indian goods is the United States (17.9 percent), followed by China (6.9 percent), the United Arab Emirates (6.5 percent), Hong Kong (3.3 percent), Singapore (3.0 percent), and Bangladesh (2.9 percent).

The ratio of imports and exports with the states of the EU is practically balanced. In 2020, goods worth 33 billion euros were exported from the EU, while goods worth 32.2 billion euros were imported. Most recently, the volume of exports and imports decreased.

Within the EU, Germany is an important trading partner for India. In 2020, the value of imported Indian goods to Germany was 8.9 billion euros. Goods worth 10.7 billion euros were exported to India. The most important import goods from India are chemical products (25.1 percent of total imports), textiles or clothing (19.3 percent), machinery and machine parts

(9.9 percent), foodstuffs (5.7 percent), electrical engineering (4.4 percent), metal goods (4.1 percent), footwear (3.7 percent), electronics (3.6 percent), and motor vehicles and motor vehicle parts (2.9 percent).

The most important German exports are machinery and machinery parts (24.6 percent), vehicles (20.5 percent), chemical products (19.6 percent), electrical engineering (7.6 percent), measurement and control technology (6.4 percent), and motor vehicles and motor vehicle parts (2.9 percent). India ranks 25th (out of 239) in the list of Germany's most important imports and 23rd in terms of exports.

EXCURSUS: THE PHARMACY OF THE WORLD

A striking feature of the imported and exported goods is the high proportion of chemical products. India produces and exports intermediate products as well as finished drugs and individual active ingredients. Even though the pharmaceutical industry in India is booming, critical voices are becoming louder and louder. These are coming primarily from the USA. This is because the standards for clinical studies and approvals do not always meet Western standards. Nevertheless, the location has advantages: As an example, a number of companies in western nations hold patent rights for AIDS preparations, in which various active ingredients are combined.

In India, patent law is handled rather laxly. In short, they simply ignore existing law and "reinvent" active ingredients. Of course, these are simple imitations, but this does not mean that the preparations are ineffective.

SERVICE COUNTRY INDIA

When it comes to services, India is a true superpower. The industry is booming like almost nowhere else in the world. The service sector accounts for 48 percent of total GDP. The country is booming in the IT sector in particular. It generated revenues of 180 billion U.S. dollars in 2019. India has scored massively in the export sector, particularly in recent years. About a third of the total revenue is generated abroad. India is not called the back office of the entire planet for nothing. India provides around 66 percent of its service capacity to the USA. The industry is growing by around 13 percent annually, and almost 4.5 million Indians work in the IT sector. There are now around 16,000 IT companies, and the trend is upward. The IT industry in India is already twice as large as that in Germany. The main advantage of Indian services is that they are cost-effective and efficient at the same time. Many Western companies outsource services to India. Therefore, it is not uncommon for American callers to end up in a call center in Delhi or Bangalore. The reason why India is able to stand up to many global competitors here can be traced back to the 1980s. The import of computers was not regulated by the government. The three most important software companies in India today are TCS (Tata Consultancy Services), WIPRO (Wipro Technologies) and INFOSYS (Infosys Technologies):

- The global company TCS (Tata Consultancy Services) is headquartered in Mumbai and generates $19.1 billion in revenue per year (fiscal 2019). Its main business activities include consulting, quality assurance, and IT service delivery. TCS helps companies with Big Data management, cloud services, SAP services, and designs tools and apps for social networks. TCS is a strategic partner of a number of major companies such as Apple, Oracle, Siemens, IBM and Microsoft. Furthermore, TCS participates in research projects and collaborates with the Fraunhofer-Gesellschaft, for example. The German office is located in Frankfurt am Main, another branch office is maintained in Düsseldorf. An important partner in Germany is Deutsche Lufthansa. Around 450,000 people work for TCS worldwide.

- Wipro (Wipro Technologies) was founded in 1945 and originally produced vegetable oils. Today, the Bangalore-based company is one of the leading providers of IT consulting and in the field of systems integration. Annually, the company generates revenues of approximately $7.8 billion (2020). Globally, Wipro is the seventh largest IT service provider and the third largest publicly traded company in India. The company has flourished since the 2000s to such an extent that one study came to an interesting conclusion: Wipro had been the largest generator of wealth for Indian society over a five-year period (1997 to 2002).

- Infosys is also headquartered in Bangalore and is one of India's largest software developers. The company has offices on every continent, has a total of 228,000 employees, and generates annual revenue of $11.9 billion (2019). Infosys was founded in 1981 by six IT specialists with a starting capital of 250 US dollars. The company was commissioned to organize the Indian census in 2010, which was also analyzed by Infosys a year later. This was the largest digitally conducted census in the world to date.

EXCURSUS: THE 2010 CENSUS

When all Indians were to be registered in 2010, this was done in an unusual way for the majority of the population. While Indians are actually used to questionnaires from the authorities, this time the Infosys company scanned the irises of those counted and took fingerprints. After registration, they were given a number; a procedure that many Indians could not relate to. During the counting procedure, in which some 2.7 million helpers went from house to house, a taboo was broken. Caste was also officially recorded. This has been considered an absolute no-go since the country's independence. Public outrage and criticism of the counting method were correspondingly high. Nevertheless, the census was successfully completed.

In addition to IT services, India is also booming in the research and development sector. Major companies such as Texas Instruments maintain large research and development centers in India. As early as 2015, around 700 foreign research and development companies had set up shop in metropolitan areas such as Bangalore.

THE ENERGY INDUSTRY IN INDIA

As the population grows, so does the country's hunger for energy and with it consumption. The authorities have not yet been successful with the task of building a nationwide power grid. There are still villages that are not connected to the power grid at all. Likewise, some settlements are supplied with electricity only during the day. The states are responsible for maintaining the power grids. The power supply itself is under state control, but generation is private. The state Central Electricity Regulatory Commission coordinates this system. Each state can decide for itself how much electricity costs and how it is generated. Therefore, there are considerable regional differences. In principle, a large part of the electricity is generated using environmentally friendly processes. India is the fourth largest producer of electricity from wind power behind China, the USA and Germany. About 35 gigawatts are produced by wind power in India. Solar energy ranks second with 25 gigawatts. Although this sounds like a lot, the share of electricity generated by renewable energy is steadily decreasing. The demand for energy is too great. To meet this demand, electricity production through the burning of fossil fuels continues to account for the largest share. Over 50 percent of India's electricity consumption is covered by coal and gas-fired power plants. The trend is upward. Accordingly, CO^2 emissions are also rising: In 2016, 2.16 billion tons of CO^2 were emitted in India. In this calculation, 1.52 billion tons came from the combustion of coal. Around the year 2000, emissions were only 1 billion tons.

GOLD, ORES, METALS AND MORE

India is a country with a large deposit of mineral resources. Iron ore, chromium, bauxite and hard coal in particular are found in abundance on the subcontinent. In 2003, the country mined an impressive 100 million tons of iron ore, making it the fourth largest producer worldwide. Bauxite mining is also very important. The country produces around 10 million tons per year of bauxite, the most important raw material for aluminum production. This makes India the fifth largest producer of bauxite in the world. Although the abundant hard coal is India's most important fossil fuel, a substantial amount continues to be imported. This is partly due to the comparatively inferior quality of Indian coal, and partly to the cheaper price of imported coal. Oil and natural gas are available, but are far from sufficient to meet demand. Existing crude oil can meet about one-third of domestic demand, and natural gas is even less important. Deposits of crude oil are located in the state of Assam, in Gujarat, in the Gulf of Khambhat and off the coast of Maharashtra. The largest deposits of raw materials are in the eastern part of India. There are significant deposits of iron ore in Chhattisgarh,

Jharkhand, and Odisha, as well as in Tamil Nadu, Goa, and Karnataka.

Although these figures read rather soberly in comparison with competitors such as China, India is by no means being left behind in international competition. On the contrary: In 2012, India's profits from the extraction of mineral resources amounted to around 29 billion euros, an increase of twelve percent compared to the previous year.

INDIA'S BANKS AND STOCK EXCHANGES

India's largest bank by far is the State Bank of India (SBI), which - as the name suggests - is owned by the state. In 2020, the bank was ranked 43rd according to the Fortune Global 500 list, which lists the 500 most important banks worldwide. Every fourth loan drawn down in India comes from the SBI. Headquartered in Mumbai, a total of about 250,000 employees work for SBI, which generates about $43.7 billion in revenue annually. The state-owned bank maintains about 24,000 branches in the country, which does not seem like much considering the size of the population. In addition, there are about 30,000 ATMs. The bank is also active abroad. There are 191 foreign branches in 36 countries worldwide (as of 2015). SBI has subsidiaries in Canada, Australia, Bangladesh, China, Bahrain, Botswana, the United Kingdom, Nepal, South Korea, South Africa, Sri Lanka and Mauritius. Other major banks include HDFC Bank, ICICI Bank, Housing Development Finance Cooperation, and Axis Bank.

Especially in the poorer part of the Indian population, microcredits granted by banks or non-governmental organizations continue to play an important role in economic development.

When it comes to securities trading, two stock exchanges play an important role in India: the Bombay Stock Exchange (BSE) and the National Stock Exchange (NSE). The BSE in Mumbai was founded as early as 1875 and is considered the oldest in Asia. The most important and best known index value of the BSE is called BSE Sensex, the 30 most important companies are indexed here. As of September 2021, the market capitalization was approximately $3.6 trillion. The younger of the two stock exchanges, the NSE, is also based in Mumbai. The most important index here is the S&P CNX Nifty, known as the Nifty 50 for short. The name is derived from the number of companies indexed. 50 companies from 21 industries are listed here.

INDIA AND CLIMATE CHANGE

Climate change is also evident on the Indian subcontinent. On average, the temperature rose by 0.36 degrees Celsius between 2010 and 2019. Although this value is below average in a global comparison, meteorologists nevertheless recorded numerous new highs during this decade. The 2010s was the hottest decade since weather records began (in India in 1901). Temperatures above 51 degrees Celsius were recorded for the first time. The effects are already showing up in people's daily lives. In 2019, about 1,500 people died as a direct result of climate change and accompanying extreme weather events such as heat waves, floods and storms. Cyclones and other storms, as well as heavy rains during the monsoon season, are normal in India, but their intensity has increased. While some regions suffer from massive flooding, other areas lack drinking water. The water shortage in the country is dramatic. In 2019, the population of Chennai, a metropolis with a population of around five million, had to be supplied with drinking water by tanker trucks. The man-made lake, which was originally intended to secure the region's water supply, had dried up completely by that time. Prime Minister Narendra Modi promised to guarantee all residents a way to access clean drinking water by 2024.

New Delhi has been classified as the world's dirtiest metropolis by the World Health Organization. A smog canopy hangs over the city on most days, and many of its residents suffer from respiratory illnesses. The main source of air pollution, in addition to power generation and industry, is traffic. There are about 7.5 million cars and mopeds on New Delhi's roads. The burning of garbage in landfills is also a major factor, as is the intensive use of wood as fuel.

Water pollution is high. Industry and also private households discharge their wastewater untreated into lakes, rivers and the Indian Ocean, including many chemicals. The Ganges is the second dirtiest river on earth after the Yangtze in China. Every year, 115,000 tons of plastic are disposed of in the Ganges, which flows into the Bay of Bengal and thus into the Indian Ocean.

Continued earth-warming is also a problem. Many Indian rivers are fed by glaciers in the Himalayan mountains. If these melt completely, there is a danger that these rivers, which are the lifeline of agriculture, especially in northern India, will dry up.

Although the challenge of climate change is weighing heavily on India, carbon emissions in the country are not falling. On the contrary: In the meantime (as of 2021), India has become the third largest emitter of carbon dioxide worldwide. The rate of emissions is continuously increasing, which is in contrast to the established economic nations within the European Union, the USA, but also Russia. Another exception is China, whose CO^2 emissions are also on the rise, exceeding India's greenhouse gas emissions many times over. In 2018, the People's Republic emitted 11,256 million tons of carbon dioxide, followed by the United States with 5,272 million tons of CO^2 in the same year. The aforementioned third place in the world is occupied by India with 2,622 million tons. By comparison, Germany is in fifth place with 753 million tons of carbon dioxide released into the atmosphere each year. The top 10 energy companies that generate the highest annual emissions worldwide also include an Indian company, National Thermal Power. The average per capita emission of environmentally hazardous greenhouse gases is 1.7 tons per year. By comparison, per capita emissions in the USA amount to 17 metric tons. Although this is ten times more than the per capita emissions in India, this figure takes on a special explosiveness due to India's high and constantly growing population.

In view of the dramatic effects of climate change, India's government is certainly willing to reduce annual emissions. Thus, the emission of CO^2 is to be reduced under consideration of economic growth. Basically, however, this is "climate protection light", if at all. Since the economy is growing solidly, this would probably not reduce absolute CO^2 emissions. Even China appears more ambitious, at least in public. Both nations fear that more consistent measures to protect the environment would have a negative impact on the current economic upswing. India is self-confident in setting its priorities: Instead of environmental protection, the fight against poverty in the country has priority. Without more power plants that produce electricity by burning fossil fuels, this plan would not be possible. While the Indian government announced the promotion of renewable alternatives such as wind energy and hydroelectric power, it is building more and more coal-fired power plants in return. The use of coal for energy production is by far the cheapest. For many years, the government has refused to accept a binding upper limit on CO^2 emissions per year.

EXCURSUS: THE SACRED RIVER

The Ganges is sacred to Hindus and is considered the personification of the deity Ganga. Many Hindu Indians wish to die at the Ganges or have their ashes scattered in the river. Bathing in the waters of the Ganges is considered sacred. One thing is certain: bathing in the Ganges is dangerous; drinking the water can be fatal. The load of E.Coli bacteria is 2,000 times higher than the (actually) permissible maximum level. There is a risk of contracting cholera and typhoid fever. Furthermore, there is a massive concentration of arsenic, lead, mercury and cyanide. In 1985, the government launched a program to combat pollution in the Ganges, but it failed miserably due to underfunding.

INDIA TOURISM

Tourism in India is booming. In 2017, the important threshold of 15 million foreign visitors was cracked for the first time. Of particular interest to tourists are the diverse culture and religious sites such as the Taj Mahal. Medical tourism is also an important field. People from the Western world in particular travel to India specifically to undergo medical treatment. Often the treatments there are cheaper than in their country of origin, or the local doctors use alternative healing methods. However, this practice of giving preferential treatment to foreign patients has come under criticism: While well-off foreigners can afford the best treatments from Indian doctors, India's health care system does not even serve the basic needs of locals. Nearly 200,000 foreign patients travel to India each year. The trend is upward. International observers expect this volume to double in the next few years.

The classic recreational vacation in beach resorts is not yet very strong, but it is undergoing a significant upswing. This is reflected in the economic output of the entire state. In 2018, about 250 billion U.S. dollars were generated in tourism. This represents almost 10 percent of India's total economic output. About 42 million people are employed in the tourism industry. The Ministry of Tourism is pushing its efforts to promote niche tourism. This includes cruise tourism in particular, but also ecotourism.

The development of tourism in India is considered positive, thanks to the many visitors who are drawn to its interesting culture and tourist attractions. Nevertheless, the country has to contend with many problems that deter tourists. These include, in particular, the desolate road conditions, which often make excursions into the Indian heartland impossible. The poor hygienic conditions are also a negative aspect. Crime in the country is comparatively low. Pickpocketing does occur, as do attempts to defraud, especially in tourist areas such as Goa. German citizens can normally enter the country with their passports through international airports without any problems. In addition, a travel visa must be applied for through the Indian embassy in Germany. Citizens of the Maldives, Bhutan and Nepal do not need a visa for entry. Most tourists come from Bangladesh, the United States and the United Kingdom. The most popular states for a vacation of foreign tourists are

Maharashtra, Tamil Nadu and Uttar Pradesh. Travel to Kashmir and the northeast of India is strongly discouraged for security reasons.

TELECOMMUNICATIONS AND INTERNET

The telecommunications structure in India is somewhat different from that in Western countries. Fixed-network connections are rather rare. In February 2021, for example, there were 1.187 billion telephone lines, including 1.15 billion mobile lines. Statistically, one Indian owns 0.84 cell phones. This makes India the second largest telecommunications market in the world behind China. This trend is on the rise. More and more inhabitants own smartphones, which is indirectly due to increasingly favorable prices. Coverage by the 3G network and 4G network is growing continuously. Thus, India's telecommunications market can become a boom industry by 2025, especially when 5G technology is finally established. There are a total of 70 telecommunications companies, making the market hotly contested. However, the entire industry is already said to be worth a total of 217 billion U.S. dollars.

Internet speeds are to be further expanded. According to the Indian government, 55 percent of households will be able to use broadband Internet by the end of 2022. By December 2024, this rate is to rise to as much as 70 percent. The aim is to establish average broadband speeds of 50 Mbit/s - throughout India.

Since 1995, it became possible for private individuals to use the Internet for the first time. Previously, use was reserved only for universities. In 1999, there were 200,000 Internet connections in the country. Businesses in particular benefited from this. Nevertheless, at that time only about half of the states had any internet connections at all. In 2007, this had increased to 70 million. In absolute terms, that is a lot, but in relation to the total population, it is a tiny proportion. According to estimates, the total number of Internet users was 411 million in 2018 and 459 million in 2019. The number of users is growing steadily.

Important websites are search engines such as Google, which record the most hits. Other important services are in the social media sector. Many users use Facebook, Instagram, WhatsApp and Twitter. News websites continue to be popular, mostly due to the comprehensive range of services. Nowhere in the world are there as many newspapers as in India, all of which maintain their own online presences. Particularly popular are dating websites, streaming services such as Netflix, e-commerce websites and the online encyclopedia Wikipedia. Websites with pornographic content are also frequently accessed. Compared to the usage behavior of Western users, there are only a few differences.

- Chapter 4 -

INDIA'S MILITARY

After the U.S., Russia and China, the Indian military is considered the fourth strongest armed force in the world and the second strongest armed force in Asia. Annual military spending was about $71 billion in 2019. There is no compulsory conscription; the Indian Army is a professional army. The individual branches of the armed forces are the army, navy, air force, and nuclear forces. According to the Indian constitution, the main task of the Indian military is to guarantee national security and safeguard the country against internal and external threats. In Tajikistan, the Indian military maintains its only foreign base, so remaining in relative proximity to the ever-disputed Kashmir region. A military agreement also exists with Mozambique.

THE ARMY OF INDIA

The Indian Army is the land-based branch of the armed forces and makes up the largest part of the Indian military. A total of about 1,240,000 soldiers perform active duty in the army. Another 960,000 soldiers serve in the reserves. The army's headquarters is in New Delhi, and there are six regional commands. Currently, there are 30 regiments, which are assembled according to various criteria. They can be formed according to specialization (paratroopers, grenadiers), regional origin (Bihar regiment) or religion (Sikh regiment). This form of regimental composition, and its obligatory commonality of soldiers by origin or faith, generally ensures a high level of loyalty within the regiments. For this very reason, the army command feared in the past that, while loyalty to one's own regiment would be very high, identification with the Indian army as such would be incomparably lower. To prevent this effect, "all-India regiments" were created, composed of soldiers from all parts of the country and all religions. The mode of operation of the individual regiments was still adopted from the British army. Therefore, it is not correct to assume that a whole regiment would be present on the battlefield. Rather, a regiment deploys individual battalions via various brigades, corps, etc. The individual formations are (descending in manpower): Command, Corps, Division, Brigade, Battalion, Company, Platoon, and Section.

The officer ranks in the Indian Army are (descending,): Field Marshal (representative title without command authority, has been awarded only twice), General, Lieutenant General, Major General, Brigadier General, Lieutenant Colonel, Major, Captain, and Lieutenant.

The crew ranks in the Indian Army are (in descending order): Subedar Major, Subedar, Naib Subedar, Havildar (equivalent to: Staff Sergeant), Naik, Lance Naik, and Sepoy (Rifleman).

The Indian Army has a large number of tanks that only partially meet the requirements of modern combat. The approximately 248 Arjun tanks delivered in 2007 were produced by the Indian defense contractor DRDO. The Arjun main battle tank has made headlines in particular for its technical shortcomings. An important part of the Indian tank army is the Russian-built T-90 main battle tank. 1,050 T-90 tanks are in service, with an additional 464 on order at the end of 2019. There are also 2,014 T-72 main battle tanks from the 1980s in active service. In addition, 800 T-55s are in reserve storage, a Soviet-designed main battle tank from the 1960s and 1970s. Furthermore, the following types of vehicles are in service with the Indian Army. The BMD airborne tank (500 units), BRDM-2 armored reconnaissance vehicles (255 units), Ferret reconnaissance vehicles (100 units), BMP-2 armored personnel carriers (1,800 units), BTR-80 armored personnel carriers (800 units), and OT-64 SKOT armored personnel carriers (300 units). There are also 750 obsolete BTR-152 transport tanks in reserve.

Great importance is attached to Indian artillery, which has been extensively expanded in the last 30 years. One conflict in which artillery provided a decisive advantage was, for example, the Kargil conflict. Since then, rocket launchers have been increasingly procured, as have 130 mm and 150 mm howitzers. The M-46 130 mm gun of Soviet manufacture is particularly widespread. The Indian Army maintains 900 of these guns, some of which have been reinforced to 155 mm barrel thickness. Other important guns include the 122 mm 2S1 (110 pieces), the 180 mm S23 howitzer (100 pieces), the 155 mm DRDO cannon (119 pieces), the 105 mm M101 howitzer, and the 122 mm D-30 (2A18) howitzer (550 pieces). Most of the cannons and howitzers used are of older design. Some of the above models were introduced by the developing nations, usually the Soviet Union and the United States, shortly after or even during World War II. In addition, rocket launchers reinforce the artillery such as the BM-30, (62 pieces), "Pinaka" (80 pieces) and BM-21 (150 pieces) models, which are, however, discontinued models and are currently being replaced by more "Pinaka" type rocket launchers.

The Air Force is currently being upgraded. One important step was the acquisition of the AH-64E Apache, a well-known combat helicopter developed in the USA. Six have been ordered, and an order for six more Apaches is currently being considered. There are also plans to purchase 135 of the Russian Kamov Ka-226 attack helicopters. 114 units of the HAL Light Combat Helicopter, an Indian-built attack helicopter, have also been ordered.

The current inventory of Indian helicopters consists of 179 Dhruv ALH/Rudra (85 more are on order), Aérospatiale SA-315 Lama (35 units) and 4 Aérospatiale SA-316.

EXCURSUS: WOMEN IN THE INDIAN ARMY

The role of women in the Indian military has a long history and began as early as 1888 with the establishment of the British Army's Nursing Service. Women worked there providing medical care. For example, 350 women served as nurses during World War II. Over the decades, women's career opportunities within the Indian armed forces have steadily expanded. However, this is not to imply de facto equality. In some branches of the armed forces, such as the armored forces or the engineer corps, it is still not possible to enlist women. For some branches, only temporary service is possible. In 2020, the options were opened up somewhat, allowing women to serve in the Corps of Engineers or the Military Police Corps.

INDIAN NAVY

The Indian Navy has its roots in the seafaring of the British East India Company. Its main task is to protect India's territorial borders and - together with the army and air force - to repel external threats. A total of 62,000 soldiers are on active duty, with 75,000 more serving in reserve. The Navy is divided into a Western Fleet and Eastern Fleet, headquartered in Mumbai and Visakhapatnam, respectively, in the state of Andhra Pradesh. In addition, there is the Southern Command, headquartered in Kochi. Each of these fleets is commanded by a vice admiral. There are 150 ships in the fleet. As of 2018, these included one aircraft carrier, eight tank landing ships, one amphibious transport dock, eleven destroyers, thirteen frigates, twenty-eight corvettes, ten patrol vessels (offshore), four tankers, one research vessel, seven survey vessels, three training vessels, and a variety of patrol boats and landing ships. India's navy has eight Sindhughosh-class submarines, four Shishumar-class submarines, and three Kalvari-class submarines. The INS Arihant of the eponymous Arihant class is of particular importance. This submarine is capable of firing ballistic missiles that can also be armed with nuclear warheads. An upgraded version of this Arihant-class is scheduled to enter service in late 2021.

The flagship of the fleet is the INS Vikramaditya, an aircraft carrier of the Kiev fleet of Soviet design. After being decommissioned in the Russian Navy (former name: Admiral Gorshkov), India bought the ship and put it into service on June 14, 2014, after extensive refurbishment. Another aircraft carrier, the INS Vikrant is currently under construction. A third aircraft carrier named INS Vishal is in the planning stage.

The backbone of the naval air force is primarily the MIG 23, a Russian-built multi-role fighter. 36 are currently in active service (as of 2020), as well as 32 light interceptors called HAL Tejas, an Indian development and in-house production. Other aircraft in the Navy's inventory include the Dornier 228 maritime patrol aircraft (24 units, 12 on order), the Boeing P-8I Poseidon maritime patrol aircraft (8 units, 15 on order or planned to be ordered), the Ilyushin Il-28 maritime patrol aircraft (5 units), and the Britten- Norman BN-2 Islander passenger aircraft (4 units). Naval aviators maintain a large number of helicopters, including the HAL Dhruv multirole helicopter (8 units, 17 ordered), the Kamov-Ka 28 sub-hunting helicopter (14 units), the

Kamov-Ka 31 early warning helicopter (14 units), the Aérospatiale SA316/319 light multirole helicopter (36 units, 6 ordered), the Westland Sea King maritime target fighter, Mk. 42 (25 units), and the Sikorsky S-61, a submarine hunter (6 units). In the future, the helicopter fleet will be strengthened by the Sikorsky UH-60 multi-role helicopter. A total of 24 of this type of helicopter, better known as the Black Hawk, have been ordered by the Indian Navy. The Indian Navy also owns a number of drones.

THE INDIAN AIR FORCE

The Indian Air Force, has a total of about 170,000 personnel. Originally, the country's air force traces its origins to the organizational structure of the British Royal Air Force. The air force is commanded by the Marshal of the Indian Air Force and is divided into five commands: The Central Air Command (headquartered at Prayagraj), the Southern Air Command at Thiruvananthapuram, the Eastern Air Command at Shillong, the Southwestern Air Command at Gandhinagar, and the Western Air Command based in New Delhi. Efforts are currently underway to modernize the Indian Air Force, which is scheduled to be completed in 2022. By then, 40 aircraft squadrons are to be assembled, comprising a total of up to 800 multi-role combat aircraft. Tanker aircraft and transport aircraft are also to be acquired. This is significant for further planning, as the range of Indian aircraft is actually sufficient to cover their national territory. However, the acquisition of tanker aircraft suggests that the Indian Air Force will also operate outside Indian territory in the future. Technically, the air force would at least be capable of doing so. For a long time, the most important combat aircraft was the

Soviet-built MiG-21, which is now hopelessly obsolete. These are now being replaced piece by piece by the French Dassault Mirage. Five of this type are already in service. There are currently 132 MiG-21s still in active service, which are now to be successively replaced by the aforementioned Dassault model. 29 aircraft have already been ordered. Other important units include the SEPECAT Jaguar fighter-bomber (130 units), MiG-29 multirole fighters (65 units), Dassault Mirage 2000 (45 units), Sukhoi Su-30 (242 units, 8 ordered) and HAL Tejas (17 units, 98 ordered). Plans are underway to acquire 144 units of the Sukhoi Su-57 multirole fighter. The Indian Air Force maintains several reconnaissance aircraft, including a Boeing 747, Boeing 737 (2 units), IAI 1125 Astra (2 units) and Bombardier Global (2 units). The AWACS, flying radar systems, Embraer ERJ-145 (2 units) and Beriev A-50 Schmel (3 units) complete the reconnaissance squadron. The Indian Air Force owns 250 transport aircraft of various types, but especially of Soviet (Antonov An-32, 104 units), German (Dornier 228, 50 units, 4 ordered) and British (Hawker-Siddeley HS 748, 57 units) design.

The Air Force maintains a relatively large number of helicopters, including the AH-64 Apache attack helicopter (22 units) and the Mil-Mi 24 (NATO code "Hind", 15 units). 65 of the Indian HAL Light Combat Helicopter are currently on order. Deployed multi-role helicopters include the HAL Dhruv (99 units, 12 on order), the Mil-Mi 8 (228 units, 48 in planning), SA-315 Lama (17 units) and the SA 31 Alouette III (77 units). The acquisition of 65 units of the Kamov Ka-226 multi-role helicopter is under consideration. Also of note are the 15 examples of the well-known U.S. CH-47 Chinook transport helicopter. The Indian Air Force also owns an unknown number of unmanned drones, but at least 220.

THE NUCLEAR FORCES

The history of India's nuclear armament began in the 1950s; the country has "officially" been a nuclear power only since 1974, the year in which the first two nuclear weapon tests were conducted. The deterrent effect, especially against the arch enemy Pakistan, was great. India is one of the few countries in the world that has not ratified the Nuclear Non-Proliferation Treaty. Notwithstanding, the country has reached individual agreements with the European Union, Russia, and Canada on the peaceful use of nuclear energy. However, the failure to sign the Non-Proliferation Treaty created skepticism within the international community, making cooperation in the peaceful use of nuclear energy difficult.

On August 25, 2012, a tactical missile was tested. The test run was successful and significant. For the first time, the missile named Prithvi-II was tested under full payload. It hit its target in the Bay of Bengal with almost pinpoint accuracy. (Scattering of less than 10 meters). The Prithvi-II missile can be equipped with a nuclear warhead weighing half a ton. The missile has a range of 350 kilometers. Meanwhile, the Indian nuclear forces have a versatile arsenal of various missile systems. Intercontinental ballistic missiles are still in development status, but could reach every continent except South America when completed. A first test flight already took place in April 2012. The designation of the missile is Agni-V.

The best-known Indian missile system bears the name Agni, an in-house development of the Indian Defence Research and Development Organization. The first test of an Agni I missile took place in 1989. The missile had a range of 700 to 1,300 kilometers. Agni-II (First tested in 1999) reached targets at a range of 2,000 to 2,500 kilometers. The first test of Agni-III took place in July 2006. The medium-range missile's range of 3,000 to 3,500 kilometers worried the governments of neighboring countries and China in particular. Because of the long range, it is possible to reach Chinese metropolises such as Shanghai or Beijing. The possibility of firing the Agni-III from submarines rather than only by land-based launch pad makes the launch site more variable and thus more dangerous. The test of the Agni-IV in November 2015 exacerbated the threat situation. The advanced medium-range missile has a range of up to 4,000 kilometers and a mass of 17 tons.

AFTERWORD

During our journey through India's diverse past and present, we began by asking ourselves the question: India - what is it anyway? Now, in retrospect, one question weighs much more heavily: Is India really a superpower? After all, the signs are quite good at the moment. The economy is growing steadily. The prosperity of the population is increasing. If we compare this with other countries - for example, with the People's Republic of China, which can confidently be called a superpower - we know that the economy and prosperity are closely linked. Once a certain upswing in living standards has been achieved, people are reluctant to give it up. Backward trends normally cause widespread resentment among the population. Therefore, the full concentration of the government of India is on maintaining the economic upswing. This is understandable. But does India's economy manage to "pick up" everyone? A major problem of the state is and remains the comparatively unrestrained population growth. The lessons of history show that a population usually settles at a stable (or even declining) level once a certain level of prosperity is reached. However, for that to be possible, a certain level of education, basic provision of necessities such as clean water, food, medical care but also an opportunity for mobility and communication has to be achieved. Not all of these aspects have been implemented in India, but the country is in the process of doing so. After all, almost every Indian now owns a cell phone, but by no means all have access to clean drinking water. Consequently, the feeling of a country divided in two is emerging. And that is indeed the case: Even though the favoritism of individual castes has been abolished by the constitution, it still exists. Even though Hindus and Muslims are equal before the law, living together as equals in everyday life does not necessarily take place in the way that the definition of equality would suggest. On the contrary, the country's history shows that religious differences led to the disintegration of the original country during British colonial rule. This was followed by four major conflicts between India and Pakistan, in effect between Hindus and Muslims. A conflict that was only mitigated when the principle of nuclear deterrence was fully established. Conventional weapons lie mostly dormant, but the tension between the two archenemies, India and Pakistan, continues to exist and revolves around Kashmir, a problem that seems almost insoluble. Peace in the region is therefore by no means guaranteed.

The fact that the economic boom appears to be boundless makes India a global superpower. But the country is paying a price for this. It is subject to the principle of forced recovery. A massively growing population yearns for prosperity. And Indian politics is happy to make this concession, rendering the country into a spiral of unviability. For a long time now, the economic boom has appeared to be overexploiting itself. The environment suffers immensely from recklessly disposed trash. Climate change is exacerbating the situation. Here, too, the number of natural disasters such as floods and heat waves is increasing. It is practically only a matter of time before the costs of dealing with these situations begin to curb economic output. The government, however, does not want to see this problem; the upswing in global boomtown India is too important. So the question remains: Is India a real superpower? The signs are not bad, but only at this moment in time. Trying to imagine what the country will look like in ten or twenty years is like looking into a crystal ball. If India is to remain this superpower on the upswing, a lot of decisions have to be made now. We can only hope that it is not too late. Ignoring international agreements to reduce CO^2 emissions is by no means the right way to go, nor are the massively failed projects to protect the environment at home.

DID YOU LIKE MY BOOK?

You have read my book and have now gained a deep insight into Indian culture. And that is exactly why I am now asking you for a small favor. Reviews are an important part of every product offered on Amazon. It is one of the first things customers look at, and it is not uncommon for reviews to later be the deciding factor in whether or not to buy a product. Especially with the endlessly large selection of Amazon, this factor is becoming increasingly important.

If you enjoyed my book, I would be more than grateful if you would leave me a review. Just write briefly what you particularly liked. It will not take more than a few minutes, I promise!

You can be sure that I will personally read every review, because it helps me a lot to make my books even better and to adapt them exactly to your wishes.

Therefore, I say to you:

THANK YOU VERY MUCH!

Your Hermann Rupold

BOOK RECOMMENDATION FOR YOU

Superpower China – Understanding the Chinese world power from Asia

Developments in China have become a constant concern to the media and society over the last few years.

But what is the truth among the many future scenarios of this superpower which operates in the shadows? How do they tick in the most highly populated country in the world? What are their aims and how does the indigenous population think? What types of developments are they making and where are their strengths and weaknesses?

Make up your own mind about this aspiring world power by understanding the figures and facts behind this expanding economy. In order to make yourself a comprehensive picture about the current export world champions, it is necessary to take into consideration their history, politics, education systems, economy and their military.

In this book you will get a glimpse of all of the aspects that make China what it is today. It is only when you look at everything together that you can begin to understand China, the country and its aims.

Super Power Russia – Understanding the Russian World Power

Developments in Putin's Russia have become a ubiquitous topic in the media and society in recent years.

But what is the truth behind the many reports about the former Soviet Union, which longs to be perceived as a superpower again? What makes the largest country on earth in terms of area tick? What are its goals and how does the local population think? What is the historical development of the country and what are its strengths and weaknesses?

Get your own picture of this former world power by understanding the facts and figures behind this historic regional power. To get a comprehensive picture of this diverse country, a deeper look at its history, politics, education system, economy, and military is necessary. In this book you will get an overview of all these aspects that make up today's Russia. Only by looking at all these sub-areas as a whole is it possible to understand the country of Russia and its goals.

Superpower Brazil – Understanding the Brazilian World Power

The developments of this South American country have become an omnipresent topic in the media and society in recent years, not only thanks to its ex-president Bolsonaro.

But what is the truth behind the many reports about South America's largest country, which is on its way to becoming a superpower? What makes the country, which is one of the world's most important food producers, tick? What are its goals and how does the local population think? What accounts for the country's historical development and what are its strengths and weaknesses?

Get your own picture of this emerging regional power by understanding the facts and figures behind the Republic of Brazil. To get a comprehensive picture of this diverse country, a deeper look at its history, politics, economy, and military is necessary.

In this book, you will get an overview of all these aspects that make up modern Brazil. Only by looking at all of these sub-areas as a whole is it possible to understand the country and its goals.

REFERENCES

Sailendra Nath Sen: Ancient Indian History and Civilization. South Asia Books, 1988, S. 164–267

Michael Alram: Die Geschichte Ostirans von den Griechenkönigen in Baktrien und Indien bis zu den iranischen Hunnen (250 v. Chr.–700 n. Chr.). In: Wilfried Seipel (Hrsg.): Weihrauch und Seide. Alte Kulturen an der Seidenstraße. Wien 1996, S. 119–140, hier S. 138.

Hermann Kulke: Indische Geschichte bis 1750, Oldenbourg Wissenschaftsverlag GmbH, München 2005, S. 43.

Johannes H. Voigt: Indien im Zweiten Weltkrieg (= Studien zur Zeitgeschichte. Band 11. Hrsg. v. Institut für Zeitgeschichte). Deutsche Verlagsanstalt, Stuttgart 1978, S. 304.

Axel Michaels: Der Hinduismus: Geschichte und Gegenwart. C. H. Beck, München 2006, ISBN 3-406-54974-8, S. 48.

Braj B. Lal:The Earliest Civilization of South Asia. (Rise, Maturity and Decline). Aryan Books International, New Delhi 1997

Swarajya P. Gupta: The Indus-Saraswati Civilization. Origins, Problems and Issues. Pratibha Prakashan, Delhi 1996,

Michael Jansen: Die Indus-Zivilisation. Wiederentdeckung einer frühen Hochkultur. DuMont, Köln 1986,

Hermann Kulke, Dietmar Rothermund: Geschichte Indiens. Von der Induskultur bis heute. Broschierte Sonderausgabe, durchgesehen und aktualisiert. Beck, München 2006.

Pengling Wang, "Indo-European Loanwords in Altaic", Sino-Platonic Papers, Hrsg. Victor H. Mair. Department of East Asian Languages and Civilizations University of Pennsylvania 1995.

Luciano Petech: Indien bis zur Mitte des 6. Jahrhunderts; in Propyläen Weltgeschichte, Band II - Hochkulturen des mittleren und östlichen Asiens, Verlag Ullstein, Frankfurt a. M., 1964, S. 460 und 461

Hermann Goetz: Geschichte Indiens (= Kohlhammer-Urban-Taschenbücher. 59, . Kohlhammer, Stuttgart 1962

Martin Hürlimann: Das vergessene Reich von Vijayanagar. In: Atlantis. Nr. 2, 1962, S. 25–69

Hans-Georg Behr: Die Moguln. Macht und Pracht der indischen Kaiser von 1369–1857. Econ Verlag, Wien/Düsseldorf 1979, S. 73ff

Bamber Gascoigne: Die Großmoguln. Glanz und Größe mohammedanischer Fürsten in Indien. Prisma Verlag, Gütersloh 1987, S. 99Ff

Prof. Annemarie Schimmel: Im Reich der Großmoguln. Geschichte, Kunst, Kultur. München 2000, S. 9.

Stewart Gordon: The Marathas. 1600–1818 (= The New Cambridge History of India. 2, 4). Cambridge University Press, Cambridge u. a. 1993,

Denis Judd: The Lion and the Tiger. The Rise and Fall of the British Raj, 1600–1947. Oxford University Press, Oxford u. a. 2004

Bernd Lemke, Martin Rink: Britisch-Indien. Vom Beginn der europäischen Expansion bis zur Entstehung Pakistans. In: Bernhard Chiari, Conrad Schetter (Hrsg.): Pakistan; Wegweiser zur Geschichte.). Im Auftrag des Militärgeschichtlichen Forschungsamtes herausgegeben. Schöningh, Paderborn u.a. 2010, S. 2–15.

Lawrence James: Raj. The Making and Unmaking of British India. Little, Brown and Co, London 19Sabyasachi Bhattacharyya: Financial Foundations of the British Raj. Menand Ideas in the post-mutiny Period of Reconstruction of Indian Public Finance, 1858–1872. Indian Institute of Advanced Study, Simla 1971.

The World Fact Book – India, Central Intelligence Agency (CIA)

Christian Wagner: Das politische System Indiens. Eine Einführung. VS Verlag für Sozialwissenschaften, Wiesbaden 2006

Five Year Plans. Planungskommission der indischen Regierung, abgerufen am 21.April 2016 (englisch).

Human Development Report 2019

Kamlesh Kapur: Portraits of a Nation: History of Ancient India. Sterling Publishers, 2010

Heinz Bechert, Richard Gombrich: Der Buddhismus: Geschichte und Gegenwart. 3. Auflage. Beck, München 2008, S. 233–347.

MRUC, RSCI, Nielsen: Indian Readership Survey. 2013, S. 8–16

Colin Clark: Population Growth and Land Use. Springer Science+Business Media, 1977, S. 44Ff

Colin McEvedy, Richard Jones: Atlas of World Population History. Facts on File, New York 1978, S. 182–185

Perry Anderson: The Indian Ideology. Verso, London 2013

Sector-wise contribution of GDP of India. Statisticstimes.com (Datenquelle: Ministry for Statistics and Programme Implementation)

Michael Kremer, Nazmul Chaudhury, F. Halsey Rogers, Karthik Muralidharan, Jeffrey Hammer: Teacher Absence in India: A Snapshot. In: Journal of the

European Economic Association. Band 3, Nr. 2/3, 2005,S.658–667

Ranking der 15 Länder mit den weltweit höchsten Militärausgaben im Jahr 2019. In: Verwaltung & Verteidigung, 27. April 2020. Auf de.Statista.com,

India, Europe Strategic Relations", Europa: Summaries of EU Legislation (European Union), 8. April 2008

Indien. 2. Auflage. Dorling Kindersley, München 2007, 34–37

Ejaz Ghani, Arti Grover Goswami, William R. Kerr Author: Highway to Success: The Impact of the Golden Quadrilateral Project for the Location and Performance of Indian Manufacturing. In: The Economic Journal. Band 126, Nr 591, 2016, S. 317–357

G. P. Singh: Researches Into the History and Civilization of the Kirātas. S. 33.

Ministry of Tribal Affairs: Report of the High Level Committee on Socio-Economic, Health and Educational Status of Tribal Communities Of

India.Government of India, Neu-Delhi Mai 2014, S. 320–331

David Arnold: Südasien (= Neue Fischer Weltgeschichte. Band 11). S. Fischer Verlag, Frankfurt am Main 2012,

https://www.bpb.de/internationales/asien/indien/189166/indiens-umweltpolitische-herausforderungen

https://www.globalfirepower.com/countries-listing.php

Fred Virkus: Politische Strukturen im Guptareich (300–550 n. Chr.). (= Band 18 der Asien- und Afrika-Studien der Humboldt-Universität, Berlin). Harrassowitz-Verlag, Wiesbaden 2004,

https://www.bpb.de/9311/aussenpolitik?p=0

Wie die Ostindien-Kompanie England eroberte | Déjà-vu Geschichte (ralfgrabuschnig.com)

IMPRINT

1st edition

 Publisher: GbR, Martin Seidel and Corinna Krupp, Bachstraße 37, 53498 Bad Breisig, email: info@expertengruppeverlag.de, cover photo: www.depositphoto.com.

Made in United States
Troutdale, OR
07/22/2024

21461041R00136